"I have lived long enough with suffering to k[now] 'one size fits all.' It is messy and confusing. Yes, G[od has plans?] for the kinds of sufferings that he sends our way, and in his remarkable book, Eric Ortlund helps us understand the various trials we encounter and what makes each so tailor-fit for us. Want to know how not to waste suffering? Here's a book that will help you discern its character and align yourself with God's purposes in adversity. What you have in your hands is a useful tool to help you sort through the complex and often frustrating world of affliction. I'm passing this book on to others, and I would encourage you to do the same!"

Joni Eareckson Tada, Founder, Joni and Friends International Disability Center

"The book of Job gives us deep and inexhaustibly bewildering insights into the power and wisdom of God in Christ. I have been humbled and instructed by this fresh, scholarly, and pastoral study. Ortlund's writing is replete with thought-provoking arguments always set in the context of an insightful love for people. I warmly recommend this book."

Christopher Ash, Writer in Residence, Tyndale House; author, *Trusting God in the Darkness* and *Job: The Wisdom of the Cross*

"If Job scares you, this is the book for you. If you feel you know Job so well you don't have to read it again, this book will change your mind. If you avoid Job because the concepts are too hard, this book will help you through it. Eric Ortlund combines knowledge with wisdom and wisdom with patience as he guides us through this mysterious and meaning-filled word from our God."

Russell Moore, public theologian, *Christianity Today*

"Suffering is a confounding matter that at some point will seemingly interrupt the plans we have for our lives. Eric Ortlund's new book doesn't try to explain away our suffering but helps us think through biblical categories of suffering. The first chapter on varieties of suffering is worth the price of the book. This study of the life of Job highlights that our relationship with God must be greater than anything this world has to offer, because eventually these earthly blessings will pass. Whether you are suffering or you know someone who is, pick up this book, highlight every page, and be transformed by the life-changing power of God through the book of Job."

Dave Furman, Senior Pastor, Redeemer Church of Dubai; author, *Being There* and *Kiss the Wave*

Suffering Wisely and Well

Suffering Wisely and Well

The Grief of Job and the Grace of God

Eric Ortlund

CROSSWAY®

WHEATON, ILLINOIS

Cover design: Jordan Singer

First printing 2022

Printed in the United States of America

Scripture quotations are from the ESV® Bible (The Holy Bible, English Standard Version®), copyright © 2001 by Crossway, a publishing ministry of Good News Publishers. Used by permission. All rights reserved.

Trade paperback ISBN: 978-1-4335-7648-5
ePub ISBN: 978-1-4335-7651-5
PDF ISBN: 978-1-4335-7649-2
Mobipocket ISBN: 978-1-4335-7650-8

Library of Congress Cataloging-in-Publication Data
Names: Ortlund, Eric Nels, author.
Title: Suffering wisely and well : the grief of Job and the grace of God / Eric Ortlund.
Description: Wheaton, Illinois : Crossway, [2022] | Includes bibliographical references and index.
Identifiers: LCCN 2021023078 (print) | LCCN 2021023079 (ebook) | ISBN 9781433576485 (trade paperback) | ISBN 9781433576515 (epub) | ISBN 9781433576492 (pdf) | ISBN 9781433576508 (mobi)
Subjects: LCSH: Bible. Job—Criticism, interpretation, etc. | Suffering—Religious aspects—Christianity. | Suffering—Biblical teaching.
Classification: LCC BS1415.52 .O7575 2022 (print) | LCC BS1415.52 (ebook) | DDC 223/.106—dc23
LC record available at https://lccn.loc.gov/2021023078
LC ebook record available at https://lccn.loc.gov/2021023079

Crossway is a publishing ministry of Good News Publishers.

VP		31	30	29	28	27	26	25	24	23	22
15	14	13	12	11	10	9	8	7	6	5	4	3	2	1

To my mother, Jani, who means more to me than I can express, who reads everything I send her, and who, as I have grown, has become one of my closest friends.

Contents

Preface *11*

1 Suffering Wisely: Varieties of Suffering in the Bible and
   Our Response *15*

2 The All-Surpassing Worth of Knowing the Lord (Job 1–2) *35*

3 Job's Torturers, the Psychology of Legalism, and the Beauty
   of Gospel Friendship (Job 3–37) *61*

4 Patiently Listening to Job's Protest and His Faith (Job 3–37) *89*

5 Job's Limits, God's Goodness, and the Continuing Presence of Evil
   (Job 38:1–40:5) *119*

6 Behemoth, Leviathan, and God's Defeat of Evil
   (Job 40:6–41:34) *143*

7 Job's Worship and Restoration (Job 42) *165*

Concluding Reflections *175*

General Index *179*

Scripture Index *185*

Preface

AS CHRISTIANS, we are told in no uncertain terms that we will suffer—it is through many tribulations that we enter the kingdom of God (Acts 14:22)—and we should not be surprised by fiery trials, for it is no strange thing for a Christian to undergo them (1 Pet. 4:12). What might be more difficult to see, however, is that the Bible portrays our sufferings as Christians as taking different forms. We suffer in different ways and for different reasons; our afflictions as God's children are not uniform. Nor are God's expectations for us always the same. Every kind of hardship should, of course, be met with steady and hopeful faith in God, looking to God's promise to bring good out of everything (Rom. 8:28) and fully to redeem his broken creation (Rev. 21:1–3). Nevertheless, the Bible's portrayal of the Christian's suffering reveals that God has different expectations for us in different kinds of trials and makes promises distinct to each. This means that part of suffering well as a Christian involves wise discernment about the particular kind of trial we are undergoing and responding appropriately.

Suffering is a vast topic—there are so many potentially helpful and biblical things to say about it. This book will not try to say all of them. Rather, in the first chapter, we will focus specifically on the

Bible's portrayal of different kinds of suffering that fall on Christians. We will examine distinguishing marks of each, what God wants from his saints in different kinds of trials, and what promises he makes to us in the different sorts of ordeals that he allows. Of course, you cannot talk about tribulation in the Bible without turning to the book of Job, the one book in all of Scripture most obviously concerned with suffering. But we will spend much more time on Job than on the other kinds of suffering portrayed in the Bible: after laying out different kinds of suffering in the first chapter, the rest of this book is exclusively devoted to the book of Job. There are two reasons for this. The first is that the book of Job reveals, in a way unlike any other book in all of Scripture, a unique kind of ordeal that God sometimes allows to befall his children, a dimension of suffering both intense and inexplicable, which has nothing to do with sin and (strange as it might sound) nothing to do with growing us spiritually.

A second reason for spending so much time on Job is that the book of Job is not very well understood in our context. Having taught and preached the book of Job in both academic and pastoral settings for more than a decade, my sense is that most Christians are mostly or entirely unfamiliar with this book. To my mind, this is tragic, because Job's story is extremely common. I have lost count of how many times people have approached me after I have taught or preached part of the book and told me they know someone whose life reflects Job's story—or that their own does. Even more poignant is the mingled surprise and clarity that these Christians express as the book of Job helps them to understand their predicament. I've also been told more times than I can count about the "help" that other Christians offer modern-day Jobs, which usually only deepens their bewilderment and pain. (We resemble Job's friends more than we realize!) God does not wait for us to have a perfect understanding of the Old Testament's most difficult book before leading us into a time of pain and loss similar to Job's. Christians need to be wise about this book if we are going to suffer well. In light of this, we're going to spend most of our time on Job.

I want to make it clear from the beginning, however, that although this book is about suffering and especially focuses on the intensely painful and bewildering quality of a Job-like ordeal, it will not be all doom and gloom. Strange as it might sound, the ending of the book of Job is one of the most joyful interludes in the entire Bible. As we'll see, God expresses a profound joy in creation when he speaks to Job, all without being glib or unrealistic in the slightest about the chaos still loose in his world, a chaos Job has experienced with such terrible intimacy. Job, for his part, heartily repents of his former criticisms of God and expresses his utter comfort and reconciliation to his heavenly friend in a new vision of God (42:1–6). And Job expresses this comfort *before* he is restored (42:7–17)—before anything in his life gets better. The joy and comfort inhabiting the final chapters of Job are really quite amazing—and they are an intrinsic part of a Job-like ordeal. Job is not the last saint to be utterly comforted, to rejoice in his very bones, while still on the ash heap.

My prayer is that just as the book of Job reveals to us one particular kind of ordeal that God sometimes allows his children to undergo, so also the profound quality of joy that ends the book would be yours as well. My prayer is that you, like Job, would be able to see God as a far more glorious Savior and friend than you had even thought, and you would be able to enter into depths with him you did not know existed (42:5). And I pray that you will be able to speak both wisely and well to Christian brothers and sisters who suffer, avoiding the false friendship of Job's friends to which we easily succumb.

1

Suffering Wisely

Varieties of Suffering in the
Bible and Our Response

THIS BOOK IS ABOUT suffering both *wisely* and *well* as a Christian. The order is important: one necessary prerequisite for suffering well involves wise discernment about the different kinds of trials we undergo, how to recognize them, and what response our Lord wants from us in each. Steadfast and patient hope in God is appropriate in every season, but there are certain times of trial in which repentance is necessary—and other times in which we absolutely should not change. God's word helps us in this. It reveals to us distinct experiences of suffering, deepening us in wisdom as to their distinct reasons in God's wise providence, what God expects from us in each, and what happy closure God has waiting as he enables us to endure. We will consider each of these in turn: how to recognize a certain kind of suffering, what God wants from us in each, and what hope we can have in each.

It is crucial to remember that the categories developed in this chapter are not airtight, and the last thing I want is for readers to trouble themselves wondering exactly where their own story fits. Life is messy, and we may not always be able to tell. At the same time, the sufferings of God's people in both Testaments are varied. Some distinctions are possible, and they are helpful to have in mind as we think about our own Christian journey and reflect with others about theirs.

Suffering for Sin

Surely the most obvious explanation for the presence of pain in our lives in the present age is our own sin. God created the world good and very good (Gen. 1), and his original intention for us was unclouded intimacy with himself and each other in a paradisiacal garden named "Delight" (Gen. 2).[1] Even if God provided his human creations with a nervous system that could react in pain for our own safety, sin and all its consequences in sorrow and loneliness and shame and heartache were no part of God's original design for us as his creatures; God planned his world so that it could function maximally without any evil being present. Indeed, part of our tragedy after the fall is that our sin and its consequences recur so frequently and deeply in daily life that it hardly occurs to us to view our shame and sadness as intruders in God's world.

It's unwise to underestimate the profound depths of human misery that exist for no other reason than our sin and rebellion against God. Can you imagine how wildly happy you would be if you had never broken any of the Ten Commandments? If you had never set up some finite good in God's place and asked it to fulfill you as

---

1 The Hebrew name Eden means "Delight" (see Ps. 36:9).

only God can, only to have your heart broken later? Never lied or cheated or stolen, never been jealous or petty or arrogant—never hurt or slighted another human being? And can you imagine how the world would change if, irrespective of being converted, everyone merely obeyed the second half of the Ten Commandments? Natural disaster and disease might still exist, but war would be a thing of the past. Police would no longer be needed—and no more courts or jails or lawyers, as well. You would never have to lock your door at night or worry about your children being harmed. Imagine if you were safe with every other human being, both physically and relationally. It takes one's breath away to imagine how much of the world's misery is our own fault.

Biblically, sin always leads to suffering, and the suffering always outweighs whatever fleeting pleasure the sin gives. David mourns the wounds that "stink and fester" because of his own foolishness (Ps. 38:5); he is sick in his bones because of his sin (38:3). In Psalm 32, David narrates how his refusal to acknowledge his sin only deepened his anguish, until confession brought release (vv. 3–5). At another point in his life, David is in such pain under God's judgment after his sin against Uriah and Bathsheba that he cannot even stand on his own two feet (2 Sam. 12:17). To give another example: the exile towers over the historical and prophetic books like an Everest as the greatest trauma of the Old Testament, but it happens only because of Israel's betrayal of their covenant Lord and persistent devotion to the gods of the nations (2 Kings 17:7–23; 25:1–21).

There are so many other examples from the Bible of sin causing suffering that it's hardly necessary to list more. Even if one is at times thankful for the connection—how much worse it would be if God left us contentedly alone in our sin, to wallow and sink forever!—a somber grief over our great sin and its tremendous consequences will sometimes be appropriate and not contrary to gospel hope. Even if it is happily not God's final word to us, perhaps each Christian will have times when he echoes Moses's agonized question: "Who considers the power of your anger, and your wrath according to the fear of you?" (Ps. 90:11).

As profound a matter as this is, however, discerning whether suffering is due to sin (in your life or a friend's) is simple. Have you sinned? The question here is not whether you are a sinner. Rather, if the normal course of your life has been interrupted by suffering, it is pastorally appropriate to ask the more specific question of whether your suffering has been allowed by God as a natural consequence of some specific and unrepented sin, with which your conscience has made peace or your memory has deliberately forgotten.

Given the way our sin and its consequences suffuse the whole of our experience, one might think that discerning whether a time of suffering is because of sin would be impossible to tell—or that we should assume all pain is (at least partially) our own fault. Instructively, however, the Bible never does this. It never guides us to say, "Humans are so profoundly and innately disposed to sin that we should assume that we are to blame (at least partially) for our suffering." The great confessional prayers of Daniel (Dan. 9) and Nehemiah (Neh. 9) specifically identify what transgressions are the cause of the present distress of God's people, instead of engaging in vague catch-alls about how we must have done something to deserve whatever we're going through. Why else would Leviticus and Deuteronomy be so minutely specific about different kinds of sin and the defilement that results unless God wanted us to be clear about what is and isn't a transgression? It's also hard not to think of Jesus's mild rebuke to the disciples who assume that either the blind man or his parents must have sinned to explain his disability (John 9:2). The Bible's insistence on the universality and profundity of sin is meant to drive us to our Savior, not to guilt-trip us into assuming that personal tragedy is always our fault.

A vague and sourceless sense of guilt is inappropriate for a Christian, and if you are suffering and unaware of deliberate and unrepented sin in your life, you should prayerfully consider the other biblical categories explored in this chapter. But when pain brings unrepented sin to mind, God's only expectation is repentance: that we take God's stand against ourselves, renounce our sin and cut ourselves off from it, offer ourselves afresh to God, amend our lives as best we can with God's help, and "restore fourfold" to anyone we have harmed (Luke 19:8).

Such repentance is very precious to God. He promises to restore anyone who will repent to fullness of life and joy in his presence. Broken bones will rejoice (Ps. 51:8); the prodigal is embraced by his happy father and feasted and celebrated (Luke 15:22–24), and heaven itself explodes in joy (Luke 15:7). When God meets a penitent so joyfully, who could resist?

Spiritual Growth and Suffering

Suffering for sin is punitive: its goal is healing, but the pain involved counts as (not unloving) discipline from our heavenly Father. But as often as the Bible shows us sin leading to suffering, there are many other examples of suffering deepening us as Christians—suffering that is not punitive but a catalyst for growth. Paul connects suffering with endurance, endurance with character, and character with hope, such that we can rejoice in trials that might otherwise break us (Rom. 5:3–4); James encourages the same joy for the same reasons (James 1:2–4). We see this truth at work in poignant and powerful ways in Joseph's life. Joseph is betrayed by his brothers and narrowly avoids being murdered only so they can cut a profit by selling him as a slave (Gen. 39:26–27). Then he languishes for two years in prison after a completely false accusation (39:20; 41:1). But instead of embittering him, the insecure and boastful teenager of Genesis 37 is transformed, using his God-given position of power and influence to bless his brothers instead of exacting revenge (Gen. 50:15–21).[2] Joseph struggles mightily to forgive his brothers, of course. But the change in him from Genesis 37 to Genesis 50 is still as striking as it is moving. And it does not happen without Joseph suffering profoundly.

Even here, of course, the distinction between suffering for sin and suffering for spiritual growth is not absolute. For example, although the exile is almost always shown to be just punishment for Israel's idolatry (e.g., Jer. 5:19), Isaiah once describes it as God's refining of his people (Isa. 48:9–10). And I suppose there would be no need for suffering that produces character if there were no sin in the world. Nevertheless, distinguishing these two kinds of affliction is valid. Joseph's suffering is not presented in the same way as Israel being sent into exile, nor the unfortunate fate of the Corinthian man being handed over to Satan (1 Cor. 5:4–5) as that hardship which toughens us up in Christ's service (Heb. 12:4–11).

God's expectations for us are also distinct: not a renunciation of past sins, but rather, assured of our undeserved forgiveness and

---

2 Joseph may actually be worse than insecure; since the sun, moon, and stars were considered divine in the ancient Middle East, Joseph's boasting of his dream that they were bowing to him (37:9) may show delusions of grandeur that border on megalomania. If this is the right way to read the dream, then his transformation into the servant-hearted man we see at the end of the book is all the more beautiful. (The fact that Joseph typologically anticipates that greater son of Jacob to whom the heavenly bodies really will bow down does not negate the fact that Joseph is, at this stage of his life, being boastful, exalting himself at his brothers' expense.)

favor with God, that we would "make every effort" in suffering to add to our faith virtue, to our virtue knowledge, to our knowledge steadfastness, to steadfastness godliness, and to godliness brotherly affection and love (2 Pet. 1:5–7). According to Romans 5:3 and James 1:2, we make these efforts joyfully, because we know of the great and precious gift that God gives us through them: spiritual maturity. John Owen wisely asks in this regard whether we have received "any eminent mercy, protection, deliverance" that we have not "improve[d] in due manner," or whether we have been "exercised with any affliction without laboring for the appointed end of it."[3] If that "appointed end" of your suffering is unclear, pray, and the same God who has allowed your ordeal will reveal to you his purposes in it and what good thing he is working into you through it. For he is indeed working something good and very good: not just moral improvement, but perfection in Christ's image (2 Cor. 3:17; 4:16–18). He is making you a Christian in complete armor, to your perfect joy and his great glory.

Persecuted for Christ's Sake

Even a superficial reading of the New Testament will show how common a theme persecution is. The apostles are frequently jailed for preaching the gospel (e.g., Acts 12:1–19). Part of Paul's boast in the Thessalonian church is the Thesssalonians' steadfastness amidst persecution (2 Thess. 1:4). Paul himself was "often near death," whipped, beaten, stoned, shipwrecked, in constant and wearying danger (2 Cor. 11:23–28). Nor is this limited to the New Testament: David was mocked for his devotion to the Lord in the midst of his suffering (Ps. 22:6–8), and those who trust in

3 John Owen, "Of the Mortification of Sin in Believers," in *The Works of John Owen*, ed. William Goold (repr., Edinburgh: Banner of Truth, 1995), 6:48.

God are hated without cause elsewhere in the Psalms (e.g., 34:21; 35:19; cf. 139:21–22). The Bible treats this as a kind of suffering separate from fatherly discipline for sin—the persecution of the early church was entirely different from (for example) God using Assyria to judge his people's idolatry and injustice (Isa. 10:1–19). It is also different from that affliction that God uses to grow us in Christlikeness: although God may have used it for their spiritual good, the many ways that Paul and the other apostles suffered in Christ's service is never tied in Acts to personal spiritual growth, but rather has its genesis in human hostility and resistance to God and his gospel (Acts 4:24–31).

God's expectation for his people when persecuted is that they would remain unflinching and steadfast in their testimony and good works (Rev. 2:10), unsurprised (John 15:20; 1 Pet. 4:12–13), loving and nonretaliatory (Matt. 5:44), trusting God to redress any wrongs suffered (2 Thess. 1:6–8), and knowing that any earthly loss is more than made up for in heavenly blessing (Heb. 10:34). We can, in turn, expect from God a glory and joy far surpassing the worst of what we endure in this life, tasted now in anticipation of its final fulfillment in the new creation (Rom. 8:18; 2 Cor. 4:17; 1 Pet. 1:3–7).

I hope no one will think, in speaking briefly about suffering for Christ's sake, that I am treating it as a light matter. My only goal is to help us discern different kinds of ordeals, and terrible as persecution can be, it is hardly difficult to recognize.

Wandering in the Wilderness

Exodus 15–17 and Numbers 11–14 narrate Israel's wilderness wanderings as a particular time of hardship and deprivation, as well as a time of particular intimacy with God. This overlaps somewhat with our first category above, in which suffering is explained in relation to sin, because although the beginning of their wilderness journey was not due to any sin, Israel's stubborn refusal to trust God's promises and take the promised land leads to forty years of wandering in the wilderness as the exodus generation dies out (Num. 13–14). It overlaps somewhat with our second category, in which God allows suffering in order to grow us spiritually, because these wanderings were a humbling test from God, a kind of spiritual training meant to teach his people dependence in the midst of need:

> You shall remember the whole way that the LORD your God has led you these forty years in the wilderness, that he might humble you, testing you to know what was in your heart, whether you would keep his commandments or not. And he humbled you and let you hunger and fed you with manna, which you did not know, nor did your fathers know, that he might make you know that man does not live by bread alone, but man lives by every word that comes from the mouth of the LORD. Your clothing did not wear out on you and your foot did not swell these forty years. Know then in your heart that, as a man disciplines his son, the LORD your God disciplines you. (Deut. 8:2–5)

Despite these overlaps, Israel's wilderness wanderings form a distinct chapter in their life with God: Israel's relationship with God takes on a particular shape after the exodus as they journey toward the promised land. The same is true for new-covenant believers in two ways. In a global sense, the whole of our Christian lives reflects Israel's history: we have been redeemed by a greater Passover lamb (1 Cor. 5:7) from slavery, not to a political power, but to those greater powers of sin and death (Col. 1:13–14), and we journey toward, not a particular geographical location in the Middle East, but toward the new creation and the new temple, where God's presence is (2 Pet. 2:11; Rev. 21:1–3). This means that all of our lives as Christians count as a kind of wandering in the "wilderness" of this present evil age (1 Pet. 1:1, 17–18; Heb. 11:10, 15–16). But Christians can "wander in the wilderness" in smaller and more specific ways as well. God can so order our lives that we find ourselves needing to trust God through a desert-like experience for a certain time. Christians should not be surprised when God leads us into a kind of desert-like experience to teach us the life of faith.[4]

Surveying Exodus 15–17 and Numbers 11–14, I see three emphases in particular that define a desert-like experience and detail what God expects from us in it and what we can expect from him.

First, the desert is where we learn to trust God like we never have before. Of course our whole lives are spent trusting God— but God sometimes providentially orders our lives so that certain comforts and structures, perhaps not sinful in themselves, are taken from us, and we must depend on him directly and more deeply than before. Israel had to wait morning and evening for food in the desert (Ex. 16:12–13) and could not store it for the future (16:21) except to avoid work on the Sabbath (16:22–30). In the same way, God sometimes allows difficulty, instability, and a kind of lack to pervade our lives in order to train us in trusting him to provide for us day by day, when other normal resources are taken from us. A desert-like pilgrimage is one in which God miraculously

4   Bruce Waltke, *An Old Testament Theology: An Exegetical, Canonical, and Thematic Approach* (Grand Rapids, MI: Zondervan, 2007), 649.

sustains us outside of those normal structures by which he normally nourishes human life.[5]

Israel does not do this very well, of course (neither do we). A second characteristic of desert-like suffering is complaining about being redeemed by God and longing to return to Egypt. We first see this in Exodus 15. Israel has just been delivered from Egypt (Ex. 14) and is soon complaining in the wilderness (Ex. 15:22–24). God responds to their first complaint by presenting his people with a choice between trusting obedience that enjoys God's abundant sustenance, or disobedience that suffers the plagues of Egypt (15:26–27). At this point in the narrative, of course, they have not yet claimed that it would have been better to have stayed slaves in Egypt—but they soon will (16:3). This means that the blunt alternative given to Israel in 15:26–27 is meant to quell, at the start of their journey, any idea of returning to Egypt. The only thing God's people will find back in Egypt is the plagues. Egypt is, as it were, part of the old order of things, under God's judgment; Israel cannot make their home there.

Unfortunately, this doesn't stop Israel from complaining about how inconvenient it is for them that God saved them and deciding that reenslavement is preferable. No sooner do they depart

---

5 I apologize if this paragraph is vague. New-covenant desert experiences are more diverse than literally walking through the Sinai wilderness; I am trying to make room for the many ways God might introduce this sort of experience into someone's life, while highlighting what I think are the defining characteristics of it (biblically and experientially). My own desert experience came about when I moved from Edinburgh to Canada, transitioned from being a full-time student (where my time was mostly my own) to teaching full-time, and had our second child. The demands on me as a father and teacher increased significantly, and the resources I had to meet them decreased. God took splendid care of me, of course, but I had to trust him and wait on him to provide strength for each day like never before. I've talked with enough other Christians who have described similar experiences that I think there is a consistency to desert-like times of deprivation, but also that the external form they take can be very different for different Christians.

from Mount Sinai (Num. 10) than the rabble among them get struck with a strong craving and infect the whole people with their complaint (Num. 11:4). It takes hardly any time at all for God's people to misremember their time in Egypt, picturing their Egyptian taskmasters as waiters providing course after course of exquisite food (11:4–6). Ironies multiply: the food cost nothing (11:5) because they were slaves, and the manna they are tired of (11:6) actually sounds fairly appetizing and can be prepared in multiple ways (11:7–9). Since honey was the only sweetener in the ancient world, the fact that manna had a honey-like taste (Ex. 16:31) makes their complaint even more ridiculous.

We are hardly different. Having been liberated from the kingdom of death and spiritual darkness, our natural home and habitat, we forgo certain pleasures and securities as we journey toward that heavenly city which is our eternal home (Heb. 11:16). But it does not take many days of doing this for us to get struck with cravings for sins we used to indulge and to misremember what it was like to be dead in sins and trespasses. Israel actually goes so far as to call Egypt the land "flowing with milk and honey," i.e., that perfect paradise of fulfillment and contentment (Num. 16:13). If we are honest, we sometimes look on our past sins the same way. As the desert trains us in trusting God daily, it also teaches how little we actually do trust God, how counterintuitive it is for us, and that we are not as mature in our faith as we thought. God uses the desert to toughen us up spiritually, to grow us in self-denial, and deepen us in our renunciation of the sins we once enjoyed in Egypt.

Sometimes suffering as a Christian involves a terrible sense of God's absence, as it does in psalms of lament (to which we will soon turn). This is, however, not the case with desert-like experiences. A third characteristic of a sojourn in the desert is that it is a time of intense and sometimes uncomfortable intimacy with God. This was Israel's experience: at Mount Sinai, a terrifying darkness and cloud and tremendous thunder and lightning (Ex. 19:16), a voice speaking from the midst of the fire (Deut. 4:12), an overwhelming presence that they could not bear (Ex. 20:19). And God has wonderful, overwhelming, not exactly comfortable encounters waiting for new-covenant believers whom he leads into the desert, where the skyscrapers and entertainments of Egypt cannot block out that numinous, terrifying beauty that calls us near and embraces us. It is in the desert that we see the glory of God. In Hosea, the desert becomes the place where we fall in love with our spiritual husband all over again as he speaks to us tenderly, alluringly (Hos. 2:14), betrothing us to himself in righteousness and justice, in love and mercy, and in faithfulness (2:19–20). The desert is the place where we know the Lord (2:20) more beautifully than we ever had before.

The desert is a time of mingled hunger and fullness, deprivation and intimacy with God. What he wants from us in the desert is trust in his daily sustenance; what he promises is deeper intimacy with him, sensuous views of his glory and beauty, a deeper enfolding in his embrace.

Lament and God-Forsakenness

Desert experiences tend to be characterized by an intimacy with God in the midst of hardship and uncertainty. By way of contrast, the psalms of lament reveal a different kind of experience in which God withdraws from the one who trusts him. These psalms bewail the absence of God, both in terms of personal experience and in terms of God's activity on the psalmist's behalf—God does not intervene for the psalmist in ways that the psalmist can legitimately expect him to. Because of this, the psalmists suffer internally, becoming sick and sorrowful. They suffer relationally as well: friendships with other saints are strained or broken (Ps. 55:12–15), and God's enemies are able to advance their own agendas to the detriment of God's people (Ps. 13:1–2).

Psalms of lament could fill a book by themselves, of course. Out of much that could be said about them, what is most pertinent to present purposes is to note that a lament is never caused by a mistake in the psalmist's perception, and the resolution of lament never amounts to the psalmist realizing God was fully present and active all the time and the psalmist somehow misunderstood. Rather, a time of lament is one in which God, in some real but not full or ultimate sense, withdraws his presence from and action on behalf of saints who trust him, exposing them to sorrow, distress, and mockery—but only for a time. The great promise in psalms of lament is that God's distance is always temporary. He always returns to the believer and reactivates his activity on their behalf. A further promise made in psalms of lament is that this reigniting of fellowship has a wonderful ripple effect beyond the sphere of the individual believer's life: God restores the trusting lamenter so gloriously that others see and are drawn into worship along with the psalmist. In other words, the psalms of lament connect the restoration of the psalmist with an expansion of God's kingdom and furthering of his purposes as God wins great praise for himself through the testimony and praise of the restored psalmist. As David says:

> I waited patiently for the LORD;
> > he inclined to me and heard my cry.
> He drew me up from the pit of destruction,
> > out of the miry bog,

and set my feet upon a rock,
    making my steps secure.
He put a new song in my mouth,
    a song of praise to our God.
Many will see and fear,
    and put their trust in the LORD. (Ps. 40:1–4)

Note the sequence from David's distress and prayer to God's intervention to David's praise in response—praise that catches the notice of others so that they join David in faith and worship. "Many will see and fear, and put their trust in the LORD." It appears that those around David observe his obvious and otherwise inexplicable return to fullness of life and joy after a time of sickness and sorrow. As a result, faithful saints are energized in worship, and those feckless among God's people are prompted to engage in real worship for the first time. This is the narrative of lament. God wins great gains for his redemptive purposes in the world as he moves his saints through lament into restoration and praise. Even if space does not permit further elaboration of this theme, a careful reading of Psalm 13 or 22 will show the reader this narrative laid out in its full dimensions. And I do not think it will be difficult for the reader to see the ways in which this narrative is fulfilled in Christ, as he is restored and raised from his ultimate lament-like ordeal, such that God wins great praise for himself within Israel and the nations (see Ps. 22:22–27; Acts 2:14–41).

Once again, these categories are not airtight. Sometimes confession of sin is a part of lament (e.g., Ps. 38); sometimes confession of sin is noticeable by its absence. Sometimes David seems to enjoy a kind of intimacy with God he would not otherwise (e.g., Ps. 56:8–11), bringing these psalms close to the "spiritual growth" category explored above. On the other hand, most laments make no mention whatsoever of spiritual growth, distinguishing them from New Testament passages that connect suffering and deeper Christlikeness. This means we should not revert to more familiar ground in seeking to understand our own times of lament (trying to understand how it's somehow our fault, or what God might be teaching us), but rather place our lament within the pattern laid out in the psalms, waiting for God to restore us, and for God to expand his kingdom and win great praise for himself as he does.

That is our hope in lament. What God expects from us when he withdraws for a time is not perfect faithfulness, but, following Christ, who has already lived through this pattern to an ultimate degree, that we would maintain our allegiance to him in the midst of opposition (e.g., Ps. 6:8), not grow wearying in crying to God to relieve our suffering, and not lose hope that God will rekindle personal fellowship with us and act on our behalf as we serve him. He promises us that these times of forsakenness are always temporary—the "how long" of lament is always "not forever"—and that many will join in our praise after he breaks his distance and silence. Many will see and fear the Lord as they see his restoring work that makes us radiant over his goodness (Jer. 31:12), believe our testimony about God's work in our life (Ps. 40:9–10), and join us in worship.

Conclusion

This chapter has been an all too brief survey of different kinds of suffering that are discernible within the chapters of the Bible. The goal has not been to say everything possible about biblical perspectives on suffering but to help readers identify and interpret their own trials, all the while allowing for overlap and messiness. There is, of course, an aspect of pain that is undifferentiated—one hurts and suffers and must trust and keep going, and there is not always much more to say. But the Bible does show that suffering meets us in different forms, that we should respond to it in overlapping but sometimes distinct ways, and that God makes promises specific to each.

But to draw these distinctions is not to exhaust what the Bible has to say about suffering. There is another kind of ordeal that God sometimes allows to meet his children, which, as we will see, is distinctly different from anything we have considered so far.

Let's imagine you are friends with a young couple in your church who have had trouble having children. One day they're overjoyed when they tell you they're expecting twins. But when the wife goes into early labor, one child dies and the other is born with severe physical and mental disabilities. The strain of simultaneously grieving and caring for their new child, together with mounting medical bills, sends their marriage into a tailspin. The couple separates, and when you call one of them to check up, you learn the wife is moving toward divorce. To top it all off, their friends at church are so intent on giving advice and "fixing" the problem that the couple stops going to church at all.

And let's say, as you talk with your friend, he says something like this:

"How could God let this happen to me? I've never been a perfect Christian, but I confessed sin when I needed to. If this is payback for my failures, why did it happen now? Why not when I was just a new Christian and still had a lot of bad habits? If it's for some sin I don't know about, why doesn't God make that sin clear to me? Is sin such a threat to God that he has to destroy my life for it?

"And if God is trying to teach me something or grow me as a Christian, couldn't he find some other way to do that without one of my children dying and my marriage collapsing? Am I really that hopeless? And if this is all to teach me some lesson, he's not making it clear to me. I haven't felt his presence in months.

"Maybe God isn't the person I thought he was. If there was any goodness in him, wouldn't he have guided my life differently? I can't help but think the further I am from God, the safer I am. What reason could God possibly have for letting all this happen? How am I supposed to go to church and sing about how wonderful God is after this? If anyone else took the life of one of my children and ruined my marriage, they'd be in jail. How am I supposed to love and trust someone who does that? And even if God restores my marriage and gives us more children, how could I ever forget what he did to me? And what if he does it again in the future? How can I ever feel safe around him again?"

The imaginary situation I have laid out here is awful but not implausible. Probably most of us know someone who has suffered in similar ways—or you have.

My hope is that as you read this imagined scenario, your mind was working to try to apply the categories of suffering discussed in this chapter but that you read with a growing sense of unease as you realized that none fit. Our imagined friend is not suffering for sin, nor is God leveraging his suffering toward spiritual growth in any obvious way. He is not being persecuted, and his situation does not fit with a desert-like experience. His situation seems closest to lament, but even here, differences emerge. For example, the enemies that show up so consistently in times of lament are absent here. There is a public dimension to lament as David suffers attack for his loyalty to the Lord, and the Lord's inactivity allows these attacks to succeed (at least for a while). But this is lacking in our imagined friend's agony. Note also how often psalms of lament speak confidently of God's restoration—sometimes so confidently that it can be difficult to tell whether God has actually restored the psalmist, or the psalmist is speaking only of his future restoration as an accomplished fact (e.g., Ps. 6:8–10). This is not the case with our friend. His wounds are so deep that even if his life were to return to normal, our friend would have trouble ever trusting God the same way again.

I actually use the above example whenever I teach the book of Job, because it summarizes many of the things Job says in the course of the book. Job will try to explain his calamity in relation to some sin on his part and come up empty (Job 7:20–21; 10:2–8). Job will reject the idea of waiting for life to rebalance itself (7:7)—no possible return to normality is a comfort to Job, for God himself has become a stranger to him (23:13–17). Job does not know what else to think except that God was not the person Job thought he was. Terrifyingly, Job starts to wonder if God is really good and fair (9:22–24).

The book of Job reveals yet another dimension of suffering that God sometimes allows, in addition to those surveyed above. What distinguishes a Job-like ordeal from other kinds of suffering is the intensity of the pain and its inexplicableness. A Job-like ordeal is one in which it is impossible to keep a stiff upper lip and just keep going, and one in which the pain is so extreme that it's impossible to imagine or even desire any return to normalcy. Any reversal of your fortunes seems pathetically inadequate to the loss you have suffered. A Job-like ordeal is also one in which our pain simply does not make sense. We try again and again to explain why we are suffering, and like waves crashing against a rock, every explanation fails.

Why does God allow this kind of ordeal to meet us? What does he expect us to do when we can read our own story in the book of Job, and what promises does he give to us when we suffer intensely and inexplicably? And, even more urgently, how can we join Job in his happy ending of profound comfort and trust in God (42:5–6), especially when the very nature of a Job-like ordeal is one in which we wonder if we can ever trust God the same way again?

2

The All-Surpassing Worth
of Knowing the Lord

(Job 1–2)

THE BOOK OF JOB FALLS naturally into several sections: the prose
introduction (chaps. 1–2), the debate between Job and his friends
(chaps. 3–37), the Lord's two speeches (chaps. 38–41), Job's final
response (42:1–6), and the prose ending (42:7–17). We're going
to look at each in turn, beginning with the deceptively simple first
two chapters. These chapters can be finished in a few minutes, but
they reveal depths in God's ways with us that few other passages in
all of Scripture do. They are both painful and poignant—and it is
crucial we understand them if we are going to suffer wisely and well.

Job's Integrity and the Principle of Retribution (1:1–5)

The book of Job begins quite innocuously, without much hint
of the great questions it will explore. After his homeland and
name, the first thing we learn about Job is his sterling spiritual

qualities (1:1). When the narrator says that Job was "blameless and upright, one who feared God and turned from evil," this is an Old Testament way of saying that Job has every virtue necessary for a wonderful relationship with God. In Old Testament Wisdom Literature especially, "fearing God" is shorthand for what we would call "Christian discipleship." It is bound up with friendship with God (Ps. 25:4), obedience toward him (Eccles. 12:13), and personal integrity in every other relationship (Ps. 15:2–4). In Deuteronomy 10:12–16, fearing God is part of loving him, obeying him, and walking with him. In other words, "fearing God" is an Old Testament way to summarize a reverent, obedient relationship with God lived out in practical ways.

We next learn how Job is blessed with what is (from an old-covenant perspective) a picture-perfect life (1:2–5). Because the number seven (and, to a lesser extent, three and ten) imply perfection, Job's seven sons and three daughters in verse 2 portray not just a large family but a deeply happy one. This is confirmed in verse 4, where we learn that family life consists of a series of family reunions, all at the children's initiative. Additionally, Job is wealthy and a man of stature (v. 3)—whenever Job walked into a room, people stood up and let Job speak first (29:8–10).

Job's sacrifice for his children is the final happy touch to this scene (1:5). Job understands that there is something twisted in the human heart that can curse God even in the midst of blessing,[1] so he avails himself of the means God has provided to make sure his kids are in the right with God.

It might be easy for modern readers to miss, but the movement from Job's spirituality in verse 1 to his blessed life in verses 2–5 is

---

1 Christopher Ash, *Job: The Wisdom of the Cross*, Preaching the Word (Wheaton, IL: Crossway, 2014), 34–36. Ash's commentary is my favorite on the book of Job.

no accident. It reflects an idea that is deeply entrenched in the Old Testament: God runs the universe in such a way that we reap what we sow, with obedience and piety leading to blessing and fullness, and disobedience leading to the opposite. (The modern term for this is the *retribution principle*.) You can see this in the blessings and curses of Leviticus 26 and Deuteronomy 28, where Israel's faithfulness to the Lord is met with large families and abundant harvests and military safety, as well as in multiple places in Proverbs (e.g., 3:1–12) and the Psalms (e.g., 128). You can even see it in the New Testament: Paul himself unambiguously states that everyone reaps what they sow (Gal. 6:7). In light of this, we are supposed to see a causal relationship between Job 1:1 and 1:2–5. Just because Job is so steadfast in his obedience to God, God blesses him greatly.

At this early stage of the book, the reader knows about Job's obedience only secondhand, from what the narrator tells us in 1:1. But as we read further in the book and see the costly and beautiful ways that Job lived out his faith, the reader has no doubt that the narrator is not overpraising Job. For instance, in 29:11–17 and 31:16–23, Job talks about the homeless people he fed and the foster kids he had in his home. He even says he went looking for people to help (29:16). Everyone had a place to eat at Job's table! It is right for God to bless such people, and it is right for others to hold them in honor (29:8–10). Job makes no claim to perfection— he was the first to confess sin openly and fearlessly when he needed to (31:31–34). There is no self-righteousness in Job. But he gives ample evidence of that beautiful combination of faith and works about which James spoke (James 1:22, 26–27). It is appropriate for people who show such unstinting care for the widow and the orphan to be blessed by God. After all, doesn't it make intuitive sense that people living in God's world who are faithful to and in friendship with God and live their faith out in loving service to others would be happy as a result?

"Does Job Love God for Nothing?" (1:6–12)

As Job continues with his picture-perfect existence, we learn that he is the subject of a very unfortunate conversation in heaven—a conversation of which he is totally unaware. Before turning to this conversation, however, a few words of explanation need to be given, for just as with the retribution principle, the scene of the "sons of God" presenting themselves before the throne of their divine sovereign (1:6) is one that was probably more familiar to ancient Israelites than modern readers. If you read other passages such as 1 Kings 22 and Isaiah 6, however, you'll notice a consistency to how God's heavenly dwelling place is portrayed as a royal court, with the king on his throne, surrounded by supernatural ministers who carry out his will (you see the same in the New Testament as well, in Revelation 4–5). The heavenly throne room is the place where the sovereign of the universe decides on policy decisions that determine how his creation is governed, which are then enacted by his supernatural servants. This means that Job's ordeal is a reflection of and connected to God's policies for all creation. Job's story has a significance far beyond himself as an individual. In fact, while Job will (mistakenly but understandably) assume God has put him on trial, it is truer to say that God and his policies toward all human beings are on trial, with Job as the unwitting key witness for God.[2]

One other point of explanation: when Job 1:6 talks about "sons of God," this does not mean God has a wife and children. Elsewhere in the Old Testament, "son of" can mean "in the category of" (like

---

2 John Walton, "Job 1: Book of," in *Dictionary of the Old Testament: Wisdom, Poetry and Writing*, ed. Tremper Longman and Peter Enns (Downers Grove, IL: IVP Academic, 2008), 338.

the "son of rebellion" in Numbers 17:25 or the son of death in 1 Samuel 20:31). These divine ministers are thus metaphorically sons of God in the sense that they are supernatural beings. But "son of" also implies dependence and subservience: these beings are not competitors with God but derive their being from outside themselves.[3] God is surrounded by powerful servants, but his own sovereignty is never in doubt. This is important in multiple ways.

Consider how eye-opening it would have been for ancient Israelites, growing up in a pagan and polytheistic context, to see their God on his throne, peerless and entirely sovereign in his rule, without any need to negotiate with other deities. It is also important for how the book of Job formulates the problem of evil: chaos and disaster are not to be attributed to chaotic gods against which the hero-savior gods fight. Whatever existence and agency evil has in the world is only at God's permission. In one way, this is more comforting than the theology of paganism. At the same time, this exalted view of God gives the problem of suffering an urgency and deepened difficulty that never obtains in paganism: while it is comforting to see such an effortlessly sovereign deity who cares for us, it becomes more difficult to understand why suffering happens in such extreme proportions when God is utterly sovereign and utterly good.

With all this in mind, we are to imagine in Job 1:6–7 that different angels are giving reports to God as they carry out his will in the earth (compare Zech. 1:7–11). The accuser is there as well and gives a report (if a vague one) to his superior, like the other divine servants.[4] Since this servant's role is to accuse, God points out Job

---

3 Ash, *Job*, 38.

4 The accuser in Job 1 is, of course, the devil, that ancient serpent and great adversary of the saints (see Rev. 12:9). The word in Hebrew is actually *śāṭān*, from which English derives its name for the devil. Readers should know, however, that the word in Hebrew is not a name but a description of a role. The word has a definite article ("the satan"), which never

to him (Job 1:8). The thought seems to be, "Here's someone you can't possibly accuse. If anyone can survive your tests, it's Job!"

There are two things to notice in verse 8. The first is that it is the Lord who brings Job into the discussion, not the accuser. Is there a hint of God's sovereign guidance of Job's ordeal as he does so? That instead of responding to an attack from the devil, God is providentially directing Job's agony for his own glory (1:21) and Job's greater good (42:5)?

The second thing to notice in 1:8 is the sterling language God uses for Job. God repeats everything 1:1 says, which is high praise in itself. He also calls Job "my servant," which puts him in the exalted company of Abraham (Gen. 26:24), Moses (Ex. 14:31), and David (2 Sam. 7:5).[5] But most significant is the phrase "there is none like him on the earth." This is an amazing thing to say because it is most often said in praise of God himself and only occasionally to describe human beings (1 Kings 8:23; Pss. 35:10; 71:19; 86:8–9; Jer. 10:6–7; Mic. 7:18).[6] This is high praise indeed! It is very important to remember this verse as we work through the book, because we will soon see that Job (understandably but mistakenly) interprets his tragedy as evidence that God is terribly angry with him. His friends do as well—but the book is telling us up front that the opposite is true. God is entirely happy with Job

---

occurs elsewhere on a name in biblical Hebrew, and the word is also used elsewhere in the OT for opposition or accusation by human beings, without any supernatural connotation (e.g., 1 Sam. 29:4; 2 Sam. 19:23; Pss. 38:21; 71:13). So when ancient Israelites read about "the Satan" among the sons of God in Job 1, they would have been able to infer that there exists a being who is opposed to God but subservient to him (note how he has to wait for God's permission to hurt Job in 1:12). But God's people may not have known much more about this figure until later stages of Scripture were given.

5 Norman Habel, *The Book of Job*, Old Testament Library (Philadelphia: Westminster, 1985), 90.

6 Solomon (1 Kings 3:12), Hezekiah (2 Kings 18:5), and Josiah (2 Kings 23:35) are described with this phrase, as is Saul (1 Sam. 10:24).

and (if I can put it this way) even proud of him, and deeply so. Remember as well that all this happens in the divine throne room. This means that the royal policy of heaven toward faithful saints is not mixed: there is nothing but love for and approval of saints who, like Job, live their faith out in sacrificial ways. It also means that sometimes God allows his beloved saints to fall into positions in which it looks to them as if God hates them—but this is only an appearance. The heart of God toward Job and every saint after him is only unmixed love and commendation.

The accuser is, of course, not impressed with God's praise of Job in 1:8 and responds with a terrible question that takes us to the heart of the book: "Does Job fear God for no reason?" (1:9; you could also translate it as "for nothing"). The implied answer is, of course, no. Job has very good reason to love God, the accuser implies—but Job doesn't really love and obey God for God's sake but only for the secondary blessings of 1:2–5. Job is actually tolerating a deity he secretly hates only so he can enjoy his perfect family and wealth and high social status. Take away the secondary blessings, and Job's actual feelings of hatred toward God will become apparent—so the accuser predicts (1:11). I used the word *hatred* because cursing in the Old Testament means more than using bad language. It means completely to reject something as utterly worthless and execrable. Job is wearing a mask with God, putting up with a God he secretly despises only in order to hold on to his fairy tale life—or so the accuser says.

Reflecting on the Significance of the Accuser's Question (1:9)

We are only nine verses into this long and complex book, but already the stakes have been raised terribly high. The point at issue is whether a relationship with God—with *God*—is possible, or whether we love the gifts more than the giver. Will we endure in a relationship with God in which all we gain from the relationship is God, and more of God? Or are we too selfish? Is all our Christianity just for show? Behind all our worship and declarations of love, are we actually treating God only as a business partner or a big Santa Claus? Can we keep the secondary blessings in a relationship with God truly secondary and dispensable? In other words, will a human being ever love God "for nothing," i.e., simply for his own sake?

Every time I am faced with this question, I feel nervous. I hope you do too. New-covenant Christians don't benefit from their relationship with God in the same way that old-covenant saints did—there is an external dimension to life with God in the Old Testament that falls away in the New Testament. While God's faithful people in the old covenant could expect large harvests, military victory, big families, and so on (see Lev. 26; Deut. 28), the promises of the new covenant are spiritual, internal, and eschatological. At the same time, however, new-covenant Christians benefit in their relationship with God in ways secondary to the forgiveness of sins and eternal life. I remember a friend of mine told me that his life got a lot better after he became a Christian because he stopped making so many stupid decisions! And speaking for myself, I never could have married the woman I did if God's grace had not been working on me for many years before I met her. But what if I had to bury a member of my family—or all of them? Would I give up on God? Would it be seen that what I really loved was my family and was interested in God only as long as my family was safe? Would it turn out that all my years as a Christian had actually been a way of dishonoring God by treating a person of infinite worth as a means to some other end?

The first chapter of Job presses this terrible question on all of us. I am not implying that we will suffer in exactly the same way that Job did—Job is not an everyman, and there is something extreme about both his piety and his suffering. But we have no reason to think that God will treat us completely differently from Job.[7] And when God allows a Christian to suffer in a way similar to Job—perhaps not losing everything in a single day, as Job did, but still suffering some great loss—and his response is, "How dare you, God! You've betrayed me!" then it becomes tragically clear that that Christian entered into a relationship with God with unworthy motives. Thomas Merton powerfully expressed exactly this issue when he wrote that "if we love God for something less than himself, we cherish a desire that can fail us. We run the risk of hating Him if we do not get what we hope for."[8]

The question in Job 1:9 becomes even worse when we consider the possibility that we might think we love God for his own sake, but our hearts are deceiving us, and our sense of happiness in God is due more to our lives being comfortable than any great spiritual contentedness in God. It is a terrible thing to learn the true quality of our love for God in the midst of suffering. C. S. Lewis writes of just this experience after the death of his wife. Although he did not have the book of Job in mind, he gets to the heart of Satan's accusation when he writes:

> Of course it is different when the thing happens to oneself, not to others, and in reality, not imagination. Yes; but should it . . . make quite such a difference as this? No. And it wouldn't for a man whose faith had been real faith and whose concern for

---

7 Ash, *Job*, 426.
8 Thomas Merton, *No Man Is an Island* (repr., San Diego: Harvest, 1985), 18.

other people's sorrows had been real concern. The case is too plain. If my house has collapsed at one blow, that is because it was a house of cards. The faith that "took things into account" was not faith but imagination. . . . It has been an imaginary faith playing with innocuous counters labelled "Illness," "Pain," "Death," and "Loneliness." I thought I trusted the rope until it mattered to me whether it would bear me. Now that it matters, I find it didn't.

Bridge players tell me that there must be some money on the game, "or else people won't take it seriously." Apparently it's like that. . . . You will never discover how serious it was until the stakes are raised horribly high; until you find that you are playing not for counters or for sixpences but for every penny you have in the world. Nothing less will shake a man—or at any rate a man like me—out of his merely verbal thinking and his merely notional beliefs. He has to be knocked silly before he comes to his senses. Only torture will bring out the truth. Only under torture does he discover it himself.[9]

The Lord could, of course, just rebuke the accuser at this point, as he does in Zechariah 3:1–2. After all, in addition to being completely untrue (as we'll see in Job 1:21), the accusation is unfair: how else is God supposed to treat people like Job, who did so much for the poor and disadvantaged? With cold indifference? Note as well the accuser's insincerity—he has to be told not to kill Job (1:12) and says absolutely nothing (2:2) when Job beautifully passes the first test (1:21). (His evasiveness in 2:1–3 is telling!) But in Job's case, God allows an ordeal to unfold in which the sincerity of Job's love

---

9 C. S. Lewis, *A Grief Observed* (repr., New York: Bantam, 1976), 42–43.

for God and the purity of his motives for being in relationship with God are tested as severely as possible. Job loses every reason to be in a relationship with God outside of God himself—God gives Job every earthly reason to give up on him (1:12). A little reflection will help us see why God allows this instead of rebuking the accuser and sparing Job this agony. After all, the only kind of relationship with God that will save us is one where he is loved for who he is, for his own sake, irrespective of what secondary, earthly blessings we gain or lose because of our relationship with him. Unless Christians can, perhaps imperfectly but sincerely, affirm the all-surpassing worth of knowing God (Phil. 3:8)—surpassing even the worth of knowing one's children—then we will be bored in the new creation, where God is "all in all" (1 Cor. 15:28). Our relationship with God must be greater than the secondary blessings he gives us, because it is a matter of time until we lose every secondary blessing when we die. Furthermore, although it is a good and healthy practice to affirm our love for God when our health is good and our family safe, some affirmations cannot remain theoretical forever. God occasionally proves the reality of our relationship with him by means of extreme suffering. When God allows these ordeals, he is not torturing us with pain when he already knows the outcome of the test. Job-like suffering is actually a matter of saving our souls by delivering us into and sealing us in the only kind of relationship with God that will make us happy in heaven, one in which we love God for no reason external to himself.

An analogy from human relationships is helpful at this point. There are some young men who will date women, develop feelings for them, and tell them they love them—but who are unwilling to get up in front of a church and pledge themselves in sickness and health, for better and worse, and so on. Men like this might think they really love their girlfriends, but they really love only themselves and stick with a girlfriend only as long as she makes them happy. By way of contrast, when a couple does utter their wedding vows to each other—when a couple promises each other, "I am sticking with you for better or worse, whether you make me happy or not"—their mutual pledges are far more than simply an expression of their feelings. The relationship between a young couple is externally different after they say their vows. They are delivered into a new level of reality with each other.

The same is true with God. When God allows some terrible loss to befall you, and, like Job, you maintain your relationship with him, you are doing far more than just expressing the faith that was inside you all along. You are delivered into a whole new level of reality with God, and your relationship becomes externally different. God is able to communicate to you his all-surpassing sufficiency in a whole new way when you affirm his infinite worth not just in times of blessing, but in times of terrible loss as well. You receive the affirmation of your faith when, like Job, you bless God regardless of what he takes from you.

It is in this that our salvation consists. Every sin involves devaluing God, and the joys of eternity consist exactly in prizing and loving and worshiping God as God. This is why God occasionally allows a Job-like ordeal for his children: he is fitting your soul for eternity and letting you receive the outcome of your faith in deeper intimacy with himself (1 Pet. 1:9). Note that this is exactly how Job's ordeal ends: almost the last thing Job says is, "Now my eye sees you" (42:5). Seeing here is much more than just gazing at something from afar; it implies that mystical vision of being caught up in the all-sufficiency of God and united to him by faith. The great old hymn "Be Still My Soul" catches this perfectly:

Be still my soul, thy Jesus can repay
From his own fullness all he takes away.

Different Explanations for Suffering and the Unique Quality of Job's Ordeal

At the end of the last chapter, I tried to define, in a brief way, how Job-like suffering does not fit within any of the other kinds of suffering portrayed in the Bible. It is helpful here to return to this point and emphasize it even more strongly, because the opening chapter of the book seems at pains to make it unavoidably clear that Job's terrible losses had absolutely nothing to do with any sin in Job's life. It is, in fact, rather because Job is so exemplary in obedience that he is tested (1:1, 8). Similarly, God is not growing Job spiritually through his suffering. Although Job never claims any perfection in obedience (31:33–34), the very first verse of the book impresses upon us that Job is a mature saint—a believer in full armor. There is no area of Job's life in which sin is still the dominant pattern; there is no virtue he lacks for which suffering can act as a catalyst to help him grow into. Job is a sinner in need of grace, and he knows it; but not even the devil can find anything in Job to accuse (and so craftily turns Job's integrity into the problem). In fact, if you read Job's assertion of his innocence in chapter 31, it is hard to imagine what else Job could have possibly done to live out his faith in love and service to others. Job's suffering in chapters 1–2 has nothing to do with making Job a more mature believer.

There is a second and subtler reason why Job's suffering cannot have anything to do with growing Job spiritually. The charge brought against Job has to do with whether Job loves God with ulterior motive, and his ordeal correspondingly involves the loss of every possible blessing in his relationship with God external to

God himself. God puts Job in a position in which he has every earthly reason to give up on God; the only reason left for Job to endure in a relationship with God is God. This means that if Job comes through his ordeal stronger in his faith—if any of the virtues listed in (for example) 2 Peter 1:5–8 are more deeply his by the end—then the accuser can simply renew his allegations, this time not with regard to earthly blessings, but spiritual ones. If Job has a stronger character because of his agony, or is more righteous or kind or more spiritually impressive, the accuser can point to these virtues as the real reason why Job says he loves God. Job simply cannot benefit from his ordeal in any way except deeper intimacy with God (Job 42:5).

From this perspective, one can say that a Job-like ordeal involves suffering that is (strange as it might sound) "useless," in which we learn to love God "for nothing." I say this because the anguish of a Job-like ordeal issues in nothing except a deeper ability to relate to and enjoy God, and is otherwise "useless." It both evokes and creates in us a love for God that is "for nothing" in the sense of loving him for no other reason than his own person. At the same time, I keep these two terms in quotation marks because of course there is a sense in which Job-like suffering and Job-like devotion to God are very much not "useless" and "for nothing"; they issue in the salvation of our souls and the realization of our deepest desires in loving union with our Savior. But describing Job-like suffering in this way is helpful in order to distinguish it from our more common explanations of suffering and adequately express the particularly frustrating nature of Job-like suffering. When we suffer because of our sin, the proper response is to repent; when God is growing us spiritually, the proper response is to "make every effort" to supply what is lacking in our faith (2 Pet. 1:5). But if

Christians are not familiar with Job but find themselves suffering in a similar way to the book's hero, it is easy for a sense of confusion to deepen their pain. We search and wrestle, wondering if there is some unrepented sin that would explain our losses, and unable to think of anything, we wonder if there is some lesson God is trying to teach us. If we are unfamiliar with the book of Job, it is very easy to start questioning God's goodness (as Job does).

But once we have a better understanding of these early chapters of Job, it becomes clear that what God wants from us in Job-like suffering is neither repentance nor deeper spiritual discipline. All he wants for us is to hold onto him—not to curse him and walk away from him, but just to maintain our relationship with him through tears and sackcloth. Job was not the last saint to be utterly comforted in his losses, utterly swallowed up in a deeper vision of God (Job 42:5). Your heavenly friend, through thorny ways, is leading you through loss and pain to that same joyful end in his own presence. If you cut yourself off from him, a far greater and more tragic loss than earthly suffering will be yours.

I am belaboring this point because, so far as I can tell, modern Western Christians too quickly turn to the first two categories of suffering to explain Job-like predicaments to themselves or others. I remember teaching Job once when a student raised his hand and said, "My mother is Job. This is her story." I asked him how often his mother's Christian friends had tried to help her by telling her she was doing something wrong (i.e., the "suffering for sin" explanation) or that God was trying to teach her something (the "suffering for growth" explanation). He confirmed that his mother had been told this often. Did it help? I asked. Did either piece of advice get to the bottom of his mother's suffering in such a way that resolved it? The student thought for a moment before shaking his head and saying, "No. That wasn't it." He knew the usual explanations for suffering did not fit but did not know how to articulate an alternative. It is just at this point that the book of Job is so helpful. It shows us why God sometimes allows suffering that is "inexplicable" within our normal categories.

Usually at this point in classroom discussions, someone asks how you can tell which explanation fits which case—how you can tell whether a Christian is enduring a Job-like ordeal or not. Perhaps the reader is wondering the same thing. I always answer by simply saying, "Very carefully." I know of no way to diagnose suffering except to very carefully find the right times and the right ways gently to ask a hurting brother or sister if some hidden and unrepented sin is being brought to light by suffering, or if some aspect of their spirituality needs to be deepened. If your Christian friend says something along the lines of, "There's no pattern of hidden rebellion against God in my life that might explain why things have gone so terribly wrong—and if God is trying to teach me a lesson, I have no idea what it is," then it's best to turn to the book of Job.

God's Providence in Job's Tragedy (1:13–19)

All we have just covered—even though it has gone on at length and we have gotten a bit ahead of ourselves in the process—has been a necessary reflection on the deep significance of the accuser's question in 1:9 and God's strategy in allowing Job's ordeal in 1:12. Turning back to Job 1, we see Job's tragedy unfold as, like clock-work, every blessing listed in verses 2–3 is taken from him, even his children (vv. 13–19). There are a number of things to note here, the most important of which is the subtle portrayal of divine sovereignty and providence. On the one hand, God is not the direct source of Job's pain—it is not God who kills Job's children but his spiritual adversary. On the other hand, the accuser cannot move until God gives him permission (1:12), and when God finally appears to Job, he does not shift the blame by pointing to the devil. This means that God sovereignly directs and takes responsibility for everything that happens in his world, without being the direct and immediate cause of evil and suffering. This is true to such an extent that the book can refer to all the disaster that God brought on Job in 42:11, even though we already know that, strictly speaking, it was Job's adversary who worked the tragedies of 1:13–19. This is important pastorally. Some people simplistically assign every tragedy directly to God, while others imagine a deity less involved and more distant, someone who perhaps can intervene but mostly watches. Neither version of God is much of a comfort in suffering, and neither fits with the portrayal of God in the book of Job.

We should note as well that the accuser works through both natural means and supernatural: the Sabeans and Chaldeans in verses 15 and 17 on the one hand, and the "fire of God . . . from heaven" in verse 16 on the other (see the same phrase in 1 Kings 18:24; 2 Kings 1:12; 2 Chron. 7:1). This means neither Job nor his friends would have thought his tragedy was just bad luck—God was unmistakably involved. However, none of the participants in the debate know about the scene in the heavenly courtroom that is narrated for the reader. Because of this, they attribute Job's suffering immediately and directly to God. They do so for understandable reasons, of course, but they are completely wrong. God is involved in Job's tragedy, but none of the human participants in the debate can decipher his true role.

It is also crucial that we understand that Job and his friends would have inferred not just that God was involved in the losses of

1:13–19, but that God was angry with Job. This is the case because, within an Old Testament framework and in light of the retribution principle, the loss of the blessings of obedience under God's hand would imply the loss of obedience—that is, it is a sign that Job had stopped obeying God (e.g., Prov. 3:33). Just as the picture-perfect life Job enjoyed in 1:2–3 was evidence of God's favor, so the loss of these blessings implies God's disfavor. That's how it would have looked, anyway. We know from 1:8 that God actually feels very differently about Job, but the reader alone is granted this larger perspective on Job's ordeal. To everyone else, God appears to be terribly angry with Job.

Blessing God When He Takes (1:20–22)

Job's immediate response to his tragedy in 1:20–21 is as poignant as it is noble. He does not suppress his grief (v. 20); there is no inhuman stoicism in Job. But Job expresses remarkable faith in God even in the midst of his pain:

> Naked I came from my mother's womb, and naked shall I return. The LORD gave, and the LORD has taken away; blessed be the name of the LORD. (v. 21)

Job knows he brings nothing into this life and will take nothing from it—naked he came, and naked he goes. In other words, Job knows all the losses of 1:13–19 were coming to him eventually. He also says, "The LORD gave"—everything Job enjoys in life is pure gift! Job enjoys the blessings of obedience purely on terms of grace, not as some kind of payment for services rendered; as a result, God is not to be faulted when he takes back what was his gift in the first place. He is, in fact, to be praised and blessed no less when he takes than when he gives. Job unambiguously passes the accuser's test as he clearly relativizes all secondary blesses to the ultimate blessing of knowing God himself. Even when it appears that God is cursing Job, Job refuses to curse back. No matter what God takes from Job, Job will bless God's name regardless. What faith! And the book of Job shows that Job was not a loser for sticking with God even through such terrible extremities. God is worth this level of devotion.

Job's confession in 1:21 is beautiful for another reason. You'll remember that the accuser predicted that Job would openly curse God if God allowed him to suffer (1:11)—but Job blesses instead. Blessing and curse are opposites in the Old Testament. This means that exactly the opposite of what the accuser predicted has happened. Instead of the embarrassment of a curse from one of God's favorite saints, God is being worshiped even more profoundly and poignantly. The accuser meant Job's suffering to break his faith and pry him away from God so that Job could (terrifyingly) belong to him. This would, of course, be a far worse loss than anything in 1:13–19. But under God's hand, Job's suffering drives him even deeper into a profound worship of God. The same is true for later Christians, when God allows us to suffer in a way like Job. God will guide our lives such that the suffering that would otherwise break and destroy our relationship with God deepens it instead.[10] In

10 When I speak of God's providential guidance in the above paragraph, I am aware that there is nothing explicit in the text that says that God is spiritually enabling Job to maintain his faith in him (that is, nothing like Paul saying how the Lord stood by him to strengthen him in 2 Tim. 4:17). But when I take the whole book of Job into account, especially the very dark and suspicious things Job says about God during his low points, I do not know how to explain how Job survives his ordeal outside of God's preservation of his saints. We will see later that Job actually gives himself every reason to curse God—but no matter what foolish things Job says against God (things of which Job will later be heartily ashamed), he cannot quite bring himself to give up on his heavenly friend. I deeply suspect God was

God's providence, the agony he allows becomes our servant, leading us into depths with God that would otherwise be closed to us.

The final verse of chapter 1 clarifies that Job did not say anything inappropriate or unseemly in attributing his losses directly to God, even though the reader knows this is not strictly the case. As stated above, the doctrine of divine providence in the book of Job is both subtle and encouraging enough to imply that Job is always within God's providential will for him without God being the direct cause of his pain. God is Job's shepherd, not his torturer.

"Skin for Skin!" The Second Chapter in Job's Ordeal (2:1–10)

One would think that Job doesn't have much more to lose after chapter 1. Unfortunately, the accuser finds a more subtle way to attack him in chapter 2. This chapter's opening scene plays out almost identically to 1:6–12, but the accuser's initial response to God's first question "sounds" different after the beautiful confession of Job in 1:21. The accuser seems unwilling to admit anything happened at all, much less concede defeat. In fact, when God points to Job's extraordinary integrity and faithfulness in his suffering (2:3),[11] the accuser claims that Job is still a pious fraud

---

secretly sustaining Job throughout his ordeal—and that he does the same for later saints who suffer according to the same pattern.

11 It can be hard to read the Lord tell the accuser, "You incited me . . . to destroy him without reason" (v. 3), because it might sound like God is admitting he was manipulated into making a mistake he now regrets. This verse is a difficult one, because the verb translated "incited" is often used elsewhere for enticing someone to do something morally wrong (e.g., Deut. 13:7; 1 Kings 21:25; 1 Chron. 21:1). However, it can also be used for urging someone to do something good (Josh. 15:18/Judg. 1:14), and once for enticing someone away from sin (Job 36:16). This means it is possible to translate the verb more neutrally as "urge." We could also understand it not as an admission of a mistake on God's part but God's statement about the accuser's motives: while Satan's plan was for Job to be destroyed for no other reason than malice, God allowed the ordeal for his own reasons. Furthermore, the adverb *for nothing* can mean "undeservedly" (e.g., Ps. 35:7, 19). This means we can read the verse as the Lord

who is only interested in the fringe benefits in a relationship with God—the fringe benefit being, in this case, just staying alive (2:4–5). In other words, the accusation is that first test did not go deep enough; Job will say anything in order to hold onto his life.[12]

As a result, the Lord allows Job's ordeal to deepen (2:6)— he seems as determined to prove the reality and sincerity of his relationship with Job as the accuser is to destroy it. As we watch poor Job sicken and sit in the ash heap (2:7–8), it is important to be clear about several things. The first is that Job is not just sick but near death; he says several times that he can feel death creeping up on him (10:20–22; 19:23–27). This is an Old Testament book, so some kind of resolution or vindication in the afterlife is not an option; the category of eschatological vindication in the New Testament has not yet been developed. Job must be as close to death as possible in order to prove his integrity, but cannot actually die. Note as well that there is nothing else to take from Job after this—no third test is possible.[13] Furthermore, just as in chapter 1, Job's sickness would have appeared to both him and his friends not just as a random misfortune but as divine punishment. We know this because the word for the boils that Job suffers is the same as the disease with which God strikes faithless Israelites in Deuteronomy 28:27, 35. Within the theological framework of this time, it would have been natural for others to assume that once-faithful Job had

---

defending his servant as totally innocent of the accuser's charge—Job deserved none of his suffering. "Thus the test proved that the Satan's accusations against Job were 'without cause' or had no inherent worth, and that Job feared God 'without cause'—Job trusted God with a pure heart filled with love for God, not for the benefits God had bestowed upon him" (John Hartley, *The Book of Job*, New International Commentary on the Old Testament [Grand Rapids, MI: Eerdmans, 1988], 80).

12 C. L. Seow, *Job 1–21*, Illuminations (Grand Rapids, MI: Eerdmans, 2013), 293.

13 Ash, *Job*, 53.

given in to temptation and indulged some secret sin, which God was bringing to light through suffering.

We must use our imaginations to appreciate the depths to which Job descends as he sits on the ash heap. He is not just unwell and dirty. In the book of Leviticus, sickness puts you in the "unclean" category, in the realm of (or at least near to) spiritual dirtiness and death, and outside of the worship and fellowship of the covenant community (e.g., Lev. 13:18–20). Ashes also have symbolic connotations of extreme and unresolved grief (2 Sam. 13:19; Est. 4:1; Ps. 102:10; Jer. 6:26). In light of this, 2:8 is almost a picture of hell: Job is in the place of uncleanness, suffering what looks like God's anger, close to death, cut off from others and from life and *shalom*, in unresolved and (he thinks) unresolvable grief.

I mentioned above how we can finish Job 1 and (wrongly) assume Job has nothing left to lose. We are probably thinking the same at this point in Job 2—but then we feel another twist of the knife as Job's wife betrays him, revealing that she has failed the accuser's test and sees no reason to maintain a relationship with God when it brings only pain (v. 9). Job's response is extraordinarily gentle, however. Although he probably could have said something much harsher, he tells her only that she is speaking foolishly and that God is to be trusted and submitted to in both blessing and disaster (2:10; note that he says "we," trying to lead his wife in his faithfulness). In this verse, Job clearly passes the accuser's second test, demonstrating he has no ulterior motive in his love for God and will remain faithful to him even when God brings Job as near the point of death as possible.

The Friends Arrive (2:11–13)

When we first meet them, Job's friends come off quite well, each making a long journey to come and comfort their friend (2:11).

They seem to underestimate the depth of Job's tragedy, however (2:12): as they gaze on their old friend, there is "something painfully strange about . . . the emptiness in his eyes, the lines in his face, the brokenness in his demeanor."[14] Nevertheless, they sit on the ground with Job (on the same level with him) and identify with him by sprinkling dust on their heads (dust is associated with death, the final end to which Job is tragically close).[15] No one speaks, however, because they see that Job's pain is very great (2:13). After Job's amazing composure in the midst of his losses in 1:21 and 2:10, it is a little strange to read of Job's inner agony; but we will soon see in the debate with his friends that although Job is entirely resigned to his losses in chapters 1–2, he only and obsessively talks about God in chapters 3–31, and about wanting his relationship with God to be healed and restored. God has become strange to Job. Job thinks he is under God's wrath but cannot think of any reason why. In chapters 3–31, Job will never once ask for his family or wealth or health back; he will only talk about his long-lost divine friend. This is the pain that (so far) he has not uttered—but it will fill the debate with his friends with a harrowing poignancy unmatched in Scripture.

What Have We Learned?

1. God allows suffering for different reasons. The book of Job is not universally relevant; it explores a particular kind of ordeal in which the pain seems both inexplicable and fruitless— it cannot be explained in relation to something wrong with us and seems to lead to no benefits. We are not better people or better Christians after a time of Job-like suffering—nor does God intend us to be.

14 Ash, *Job*, 60–61.
15 Ash, *Job*, 61.

2. God sometimes allows Job-like ordeals, not because he is angry with us or trying to teach us a lesson but in order to prove the reality of our relationship with him. God sometimes puts us in a position where we lose every earthly reason to be in a relationship with him. This is because there is no other way to deliver us into the kind of relationship with himself where he is loved and honored simply for his own sake. This is the only kind of relationship with God that honors God as *God* and which will make us happy in eternity. Job-like suffering and loss is, at the end of the day, a means for God to work the salvation of our souls. Only in a Job-like ordeal do we experience the all-sufficiency of God himself as a reality, not a theory. If God is going to save us, he can do nothing else.

3. What God wants from us in Job-like ordeals is not to repent or grow but simply to hold on to him. That's it. We will probably say some foolish things along the way, of which we are later ashamed (see Job 42:6); but God will be gentle with us in our ordeal. His only requirement is not to curse him.

4. Although God sovereignly directs everything in his universe, he is not the direct and immediate source of all evil. Even when it may not feel like it, you are really safe with God—nothing can touch you without his permission, and his own disposition toward you and plans for you are only always for your good.

5. In God's providence, the evil he allows to touch your life will have exactly the opposite effect of what your spiritual adversary intends—instead of destroying your faith, it will drive you deeper into worship.

6. One dimension of a Job-like ordeal involves a huge disparity between how things appear to us and what our true status and standing is in the eyes of God. God is unambiguously proud of Job (1:8); but part of Job's ordeal involves putting him in a position in which Job has every evidence that God is terribly angry with him and putting him under a curse. The reader learns far more about what was really happening in Job's case than Job ever does. In the same way, Job-like suffering involves a sickening confusion that comes from obsessively trying to lessen our pain by understanding or explaining it, and always failing. When we find ourselves in a Job-like ordeal, we will never fully understand all the factors at play. But the larger heavenly perspective of Job 1–2 is meant to give us hope: even when it looks like you have empirical evidence that God has given up on you, God's heart toward you is entirely different. God is so proud of Job he bragged about him to the devil—and in Christ, he's bragging to the devil about you too.

3

Job's Torturers, the Psychology of Legalism, and the Beauty of Gospel Friendship

(Job 3–37)

ONE OF THE WAYS in which the book of Job is unique in the Bible is its focus on wise speech in the midst of suffering. Other theodicy texts in the Old Testament, such as Habakkuk or Psalm 73, will show an overlap with themes in Job, but the book of Job is the one place in the Bible that specifically examines how to speak in healing ways to those who are suffering. In fact, the speeches that Job and his friends make to each other take up about four-fifths of the entire book! This is our focus in this chapter: having learned why God sometimes allows Job-like ordeals and what he wants from us in them, we turn to consider how we should speak to inexplicable suffering—and how we can avoid the fate of the friends, who fell under God's terrible anger and required the intercession of their better (42:8).

Fortunately, despite the fact that it takes up the majority of the book of Job, the debate between Job and his friends is very simple to summarize.[1] All members of the debate are convinced that God is angry at Job. We saw in the last chapter that even though they are completely mistaken about God's heart toward Job, the only inference Job and his friends can draw with their limited understanding of Job's situation and within their (not entirely wrong) theological framework is that Job is being punished by God as a sinner. The single disagreement among them is whether God has good reason to be angry. The friends are convinced that because God is just and fair, he would not punish Job without cause. Even if they cannot see it, they are certain that Job must have engaged in hidden and unrepentant sin. Job, on the other hand, knows he has not compromised and started to lead a double life. He knows he has done nothing to deserve being put in the "sinner" category. This means that he cannot explain his tragedy in relation to himself—and as a result, he finds himself pushed to explain it in relation to God. Job doesn't know what else to think except that God must not be good and fair. Unwillingly, he starts to utter some very sinister suspicions about God's character as he tries to explain his tragedy.

As we will see, Job also expresses remarkable faith in the God he no longer entirely trusts—but Job's speeches are agonized and involved enough that I am going to leave them for the next chapter and focus only on Job's friends here. As we do, we will see that while Eliphaz, Bildad, and Zophar appear initially plausible and even helpful—and while we would naturally side with them if we

---

1 This means that we will not work our way carefully through every part of the friends' speeches, as we did with chaps. 1–2. This book is not an exhaustive study of every chapter in the book of Job. For those interested in more, I recommend starting with Christopher Ash's *Job: The Wisdom of the Cross*, Preaching the Word (Wheaton, IL: Crossway, 2014).

were not given the insight into Job's predicament, which chapters 1–2 reveal—Job's friends are actually his tormentors, and no matter how much stage time they are given, they cannot manage to say a single helpful thing to him. As we wade through chapter after chapter of bombastic, moralistic condemnation, their speeches quickly become very frustrating to read. My sense is, however, that this is exactly what the Joban poet intends and that he records the friends' speeches to show us what *not* to say to suffering brothers and sisters. Furthermore, I suspect that one of the reasons that the poet lets the debate go on for so long is to provoke such disgust at the friends that we resolve never to speak to a modern-day Job in the same way. The author is trying to inoculate us against this way of thinking and speaking.

It is important that he do so, because the kind of theology and pastoral council represented by Eliphaz and his friends is actually very common and (at a superficial level) easy to agree with—so common, in fact, that we've probably said similar things at one time or another. The narrator is aware of this, and part of his genius is to show us an initial and superficial plausibility to the friends' words—only to let us watch as the friends quickly discredit themselves and spend most of the book being completely infuriating. This means that as our initial sympathy turns to frustration, we are supposed to be humbled and chastened too. "How forceful are upright words!" Job complains (6:25)—but as we read, we are supposed to worry that we can be just as forceful. Our frustration with the friends should simultaneously be directed at ourselves.

Being humbled and chastened is not enough, however. We need more than negative examples. What *should* we say to a Christian undergoing a Job-like ordeal? The book of Job does not explicitly answer this question, but the outline of an answer is present, revealed in the shape of the scars left of the friends' hellish comforts. We'll attempt to articulate what this answer might look like at the end of this chapter.

Let's begin by looking at Eliphaz's first speech, its initial plausibility, and its horrible implications.

Eliphaz's Hideous Gentleness (Job 4)

Eliphaz begins with admirable tact: we can read 4:2 as Eliphaz saying (quietly, gently), "Job, would it be possible for me to speak? Is that all right? After all, something has to be said." Eliphaz is right: sitting in the ash heap with his sick friend, with the graves of Job's ten children standing nearby, one cannot remain silent forever. Eliphaz addresses his suffering friend by pointing to Job's impressive past record of helping others who were suffering (4:3–4). But now "it" comes upon Job, and Job is impatient and dismayed (4:5)— Eliphaz does not say so, but he is referring here to Job's losses in chapters 1–2 as well as Job's curse on creation in chapter 3, which we will consider in the next chapter.[2] And yet, Eliphaz implies, Job's curse is an overreaction. Job does not need to engage in the agonized hysterics of wishing he had never been born. He already knows what to do because he has helped others in exactly the same situation. There is a hope and a confidence for Job—all found in fearing God and personal integrity (4:6).

Eliphaz is delicately saying less than he thinks here, letting Job draw the right conclusion without shaming his friend by being too blunt. (He'll save that strategy for later chapters.) We don't have to read too much between the lines of 4:3–6, however, to flesh out

---

2   The NIV overtranslates this verse by adding "trouble." This correctly discerns Eliphaz's meaning—he is referring to Job's tragedy in chaps. 1–2—but the word is not in the Hebrew. Eliphaz is trying to be polite and understated.

Eliphaz's pastoral counseling strategy for Job. Eliphaz is implying that Job has abandoned the fear of God and given up on personal integrity (v. 6); as a result, suffering has come upon him (v. 5), the same suffering for sin from which he helped other penitents recover through repentance (vv. 3–4). Job himself knows what to do; Eliphaz is only reminding Job of what he has taught others.

At first, all this seems very sensible, very tactful. But it is at exactly this point that the perceptive reader feels his first doubt about Eliphaz. This is because the "fear of God" and "integrity of . . . ways" to which he refers in 4:6 have already come up in the book of Job—in the very first verse of the book, where we learned that Job has these qualities to an outstanding degree. We know something that the characters in the book do not—it is absolutely not because Job has lost these qualities that he is suffering but because he possesses them so deeply. Eliphaz has interpreted Job's situation exactly wrongly. But at the same time we realize this, we also realize that it is entirely natural, within Eliphaz's limited perspective, for him to draw these terribly mistaken conclusions about Job. Eliphaz does not know Job's true state before God, and there is no way he can learn what he does not know; he is ignorant about his own ignorance. He has every reason to think Job's case is quite simple, and he expects his advice to be received gratefully by Job.

This produces an odd effect as we read Eliphaz and the other friends. On the one hand, we understand why they draw the conclusion they do; but the more they press this conclusion on Job, the less we trust them. You can see this in the very next verse, where Eliphaz says that God will not give up on innocent people, leaving them to destitution or death (4:7). Job is sick unto death as he hears these words (2:7). This means that Eliphaz is addressing 4:7 directly to Job, even though he, politely, does not say so. He is implying that it is because Job has lost his innocence that he is close to death. But the reader knows this is simply not true. At the same time, there are verses elsewhere in the Old Testament that are similar to Job 4:7. Psalm 37:9 is a prominent example, and it even uses similar language to Job 4:7. So while Eliphaz has some scriptural backing in his favor, we also know he is misapplying a scriptural truth in a way he cannot see.

Eliphaz is, however, completely confident of this misapplication. In 4:8, he begins his summary of the retribution principle by saying, "I have seen"—that is, he has personally witnessed that everyone reaps what they sow. Surely Eliphaz is not the only person to have observed this. Probably many of us have witnessed how foolish and sinful decisions reap bitter consequences. Again, we sympathize. Eliphaz adds to this that no one is exempt from this pattern in God's ordering of the world—though a sinner be fierce and indomitable as a lion, no one can escape the law of retribution (4:9–11). And I suppose it's hard to fault Eliphaz for thinking this. Is it at all plausible to think that some human beings can, through mere willpower and craftiness, thumb their nose at God and get away with it? Of course not. But even as we concede these points to Eliphaz, we cannot forget what we learned about Job from chapters 1–2. In a way Eliphaz does not and cannot know, Job is very much not reaping what he has sown. All Eliphaz's well-intentioned advice is at best irrelevant (at best).

Eliphaz takes a different tack in 4:11–21. It turns out that Eliphaz has a bit of a charismatic streak: he recently had a spiritual experience, a message from the beyond, which he's certain will be helpful to Job. Eliphaz takes five verses to describe the experience (vv. 12–16) and another five to give the message he received (vv. 17–21). There is perhaps a note of pride in verse 12: he says (literally) a word was "stolen" (translated as "brought to me stealthily"). I wonder if he feels privileged to have had access to an insight denied to others. Dreams are, of course, a valid mode of revelation in the Old Testament (e.g., Gen. 40–41; Joel 3:1). Furthermore, without at all discounting the Bible as our ultimate authority, I don't want to rule out God speaking to his children in a variety of ways—whether through dreams or the words of a friend. In light of this, there is nothing wrong in principle with Eliphaz speaking to Job on the basis of this experience. But as we read Eliphaz's account, doubts again spring up about this strange encounter and about Eliphaz for accepting it so uncritically. Eliphaz is shaking with fear (4:14) in the darkest hour of the night (4:13) as a spirit appears to him that won't quite come into focus (4:15). Even though being troubled by dreams and visions happens elsewhere in the Old Testament (such as Dan. 7:28; 8:27), no other dream is so spooky or sinister as this. It almost sounds like a scene from a horror movie. One commentator went so far as to call this passage a parody of revelatory dreams.[3] Is this really from God?

What the spirit says raises even more doubts. Can a man be right before God? it asks (4:17). As Christians reading the book, we are so used to calling ourselves sinners before God—and rightly so—that we might be tempted to answer no. But to do so is slightly to misunderstand the question. All of this is directed at Job, whom we have already seen makes no pretension to perfect sinlessness (see 31:33–34) and relates to God on terms of grace, not any presumption of merit (remember the theology of grace in 1:21). The question in 4:17 is not, Are all people naturally sinners and in need of God's grace? The question is rather, Can any human being

---

3 Norman Habel, *The Book of Job*, Old Testament Library (Louisville, KY: Westminster John Knox, 1985), 123.

ever be on good terms with God? Is it at all possible for men and women to stand in a right relationship with their Creator? The answer to this question is obviously yes, and Job himself is prime evidence of this (1:1, 8). But the answer implied by this spirit is no. According to this spirit, God is the great finger pointer and blamer, who can find some fault with each one of his servants—even his divine ones (4:18). And if even angels are disappointing to God, humans must be even more so, who are described metaphorically as dwelling in houses of clay, so weak that even a moth's wing crushes them (4:19–21).

Therefore, Job is guilty. Everyone is—God says so. So Job deserved everything he got in chapters 1–2. Eliphaz has personally witnessed that people reap what they sow (4:8); his eerie mystical experience confirms it.

There are several things to notice as we read this. To begin with, I'm not sure how consistent the theology of chapter 4 is. After all, if everyone stands under God's displeasure (vv. 18–21), how can Eliphaz's precious retribution principle work in anyone's favor? Isn't everyone destined for punishment? Eliphaz does not talk about grace in his speeches, so he must attribute incredible power to repentance as a way to clean oneself up and make oneself presentable to God. But this is very different from the Bible's portrayal of repentance (see Luke 18:13–14).

Note as well that when the spirit says that God puts no trust in his servants, this creates another echo to chapter 1, where God named Job his servant (1:8). In light of this, it is simply false to say that God puts no trust in his servants, as this spirit claims in 4:18. After all, even if God does not trust Job in the sense of depending on him, God does entrust his reputation to Job, at least in the sense that God's reputation will be lessened if his favorite servant curses him and enhanced when Job does not (1:21). In light of this, 4:18 is flatly false. This casts suspicion on everything else the spirit says.

Finally, when we read of a spirit who portrays God as the great condemner, who finds fault even with his angels, it is hard not to wonder who this spirit might be. We are not explicitly told, of course—but perhaps the reader has already started to wonder if the accuser from chapter 1 has managed to reinsert himself in the story and find another way to torture Job, this time not through his wife (2:9) but through a well-intentioned friend. Although we cannot be certain, it would make a lot of sense for the devil, embittered and still rebellious, to portray God diametrically opposite to the loving and faithful friend he really is, in order to try yet again to destroy Job's faith. Poor Job! Just when you think he cannot possibly suffer any more, there is another twist of the knife. And there may be a sense in which this is the most cruel twist of all: how do you think it felt for Job, who loved God so profoundly, to be told by a trusted friend that God was terribly disappointed in him and punishing him in anger? And that God was right to do so?

The thing we must not miss in chapter 4 is that Eliphaz, despite his good intentions, despite his pastoral tact, despite the fact that he has empirical evidence (v. 8) for thinking as he does, evidence that is complemented by a mystical experience (vv. 11–12), and even despite the fact that he has some scriptural backing, is not only completely misinterpreting Job's situation—he is acting as a mouthpiece for the devil as he does. He is passing on condemnation from the mouth of hell, all the while convinced he is speaking on God's behalf and doing Job a favor. If that fails to provoke in us a humility with each other, a gentleness, a self-suspicion, an unwillingness to condemn, nothing will.

Eliphaz's Theology and His Crucial Mistake (Job 5)

In the comments I have made so far, I have said that Eliphaz has some scriptural support for the theological framework he uses to condemn Job. This has probably raised some questions: if Eliphaz can, in some sense, invoke Scripture in support of his theology, where exactly has he gone wrong? To answer this, let's survey chapter 5, with an eye to Eliphaz's two later speeches in chapters 15 and 22. In chapter 5, Eliphaz tries to convince Job that Job has everything to gain and nothing to lose by repenting of whatever secret sin has provoked God's just anger. Eliphaz begins with the judgment of the wicked (5:1–7), implying that Job belongs in that category as long as he refuses to repent: "vexation kills the fool," he says (5:2), so Job should not be vexed at his punishment but rather repent. (By the way, don't miss how verse 4 is a spectacularly graceless thing to say to someone whose children are dead.) But if God judges the wicked (5:11–14), he just as easily saves the helpless (5:15–16); in light of this, Job should penitently seek God (5:8). The very brightest of futures awaits Job if he will do so (5:18–27; remember that this is the future Eliphaz sincerely wants for his friend). The one thing Job must avoid is fighting God's judgment—resisting the justice God has brought down on Job's head (5:17). The tragedy of chapters 1–2 is fatherly discipline from God for sin, Eliphaz says; but if Job admits he got what he deserved, the principle of retribution will work in his favor in the most beautiful of ways (5:19–26).

Readers familiar with the Old Testament will recognize that 5:17 sounds very similar to what the wise father tells his son in Proverbs 3:11–12. These verses are also applied to new-covenant believers in Hebrews 12:3–11. This is not the only point of contact between

Eliphaz's speech in chapter 5 and the rest of the Old Testament; 5:9 is similar to Psalm 40:5, for example, and 5:10 finds echoes in Psalm 65:9–10, while 5:11 sounds a lot like 1 Samuel 2:7–8. And it is true, of course, that God does things great and unsearchable, marvelous and without number, for those who seek him (5:8–9). So where exactly has Eliphaz gone wrong?

Although it is only implicit in Job 4–5, it will quickly become clear that while the principle of retribution is taught elsewhere in Scripture, Eliphaz and his friends have overinterpreted it in a narrow and mechanistic way to the point that even when they summarize the idea in a way that sounds true (as in 4:8), their version of that principle is so far from the biblical one as to be false. This becomes clearer as the book progresses. For example, if you read the second half of Eliphaz's second speech in 15:17–35, you'll see how each line of poetry in this passage neatly dispatches the wicked—as soon as each domino is set up, Eliphaz knocks it down. Eliphaz portrays the world as if bad people are dispatched always instantly. He also says that "the wicked man writhes in pain all his days" (15:20) and his sin is paid back "in full before his time" (15:32)—a completely unrealistic description of how God's justice gets worked out in the world.

Now, the rest of the Bible, along with the book of Job itself, does affirm that everyone reaps what they sow (Gal. 6:7). Even Job's story ends in blessing, not in destitution (42:10–17). This means that the book of Job itself affirms the retribution principle, because Job's story ends with him reaping the benefits of his faithfulness and integrity with God. It is important to affirm this as strongly as the Bible does, because God is teaching us that following him is really worth it in the end, no matter what suffering it costs us along the way.

But it is equally important to affirm that Scripture teaches the principle of retribution in a general and long-term way. It never teaches that we reap what we sow in the immediate, obvious, domino-like fashion that Eliphaz and his friends imagine. As an example, note how neither righteous Naboth (1 Kings 21) nor sinful Israel (2 Kings 14:23–27) reaps what is sown—not in a quick or obvious way at least. And it is this that the friends will not allow. They see such a tight and even mechanistic connection between good behavior and reward that they think they can infer backward from reward to good behavior—and from suffering to bad behavior. Contradicting this, a major part of the wisdom of the book of Job teaches us that although God does deeply bless faithfulness to himself, he reserves the right to temporarily interrupt this pattern for his own reasons. In other words, it is true that you reap what you sow, but it is not true to say that you reap only what you sow. Suffering and loss can meet God's imperfect but sincere saints in such a way that cannot be explained with reference to their past sins and failures. Sometimes suffering meets us, but not because we have sown it. The pattern of retribution ultimately holds true in God's universe—but not in a quick or automatic way.

The friends will have none of this. For them, undeserved suffering is a contradiction in terms,[4] and any statement to the contrary is attacked with sustained and vicious polemics. It is even attacked in ridiculous ways: in 22:5–11, Eliphaz goes so far as to invent a catalogue of sins that Job has supposedly committed. Abandoning all pretense of pastoral sensitivity, Eliphaz angrily blasts Job as someone exploiting the poor for his own advantage. But we have known from the very first verse of the book that this is not true!

---

4 As pointed out by Åke Viberg, "Job," in *New Dictionary of Biblical Theology*, ed. T. Desmond Alexander and Brian Rosner (Downers Grove, IL: InterVarsity Press, 2004), 202.

Why is Eliphaz insisting so strongly on the ridiculous claim that Job's evil is abundant, open, and obvious (22:5)? At the beginning of the debate in chapters 4–5, Eliphaz might be forgiven for drawing the wrong conclusion. But as Job insists that he did nothing to deserve being treated as a sinner by God and that he wants to speak sincerely and honestly with his friends (6:28–30), Eliphaz has an opportunity to reevaluate and engage with Job in a different way. Instead, he refuses and doubles down on how evil Job is, even going to the bizarre extreme of inventing sins so that he can condemn Job. Why is Eliphaz so blindly and neurotically committed to his shallow version of the retribution principle?

The Psychology of Legalism and the Temptation to Blame

We can infer an answer to this question from 15:4, in which Eliphaz makes a significant blunder. In this verse, Eliphaz accuses Job of "doing away with the fear of God and hindering meditation before God." This is in response to Job's repeated insistence that he has done nothing to deserve what looks like the punishment of chapters 1–2 (see 6:10; 13:15–16). Eliphaz hears Job's insistence on innocence and responds by claiming that Job is destroying real spirituality—if Job is right, everyone will (to use modern terms) stop going to church, reading their Bible, following God, giving to the poor, and so on.

At first glance, this is a strange conclusion to draw, but a moment's reflection reveals what Eliphaz is thinking. Eliphaz's worry is that if it gets out that Job really is innocent and is suffering regardless—if it is possible to serve God scrupulously for decades and have it, as it were, count for nothing—then no one will serve God at all. The unstated premise here is that people only get into a relationship with God for the blessings that accrue to obedience;

otherwise (Eliphaz thinks) we are serving God for no reason. But if it is possible that someone can serve God and not be blessed for it—i.e., if Job is innocent and still suffering—Eliphaz assumes everyone will lose their motivation for serving God in the first place. As a result, Eliphaz must condemn and smear Job.

I have tried to sketch Eliphaz's thought in such a way that alludes to the accuser's question in 1:9, because, although he does not say so, Eliphaz gives no indication of loving God purely for his own sake. It does not seem to occur to Eliphaz that Job or anyone else might love God "for nothing," irrespective of secondary blessings gained or lost. For this reason, I do not think Eliphaz or the other friends would have passed the accuser's test. You see this in the way the friends say less and less about God as the book proceeds. God becomes distant in the friends' later speeches and seems to exist mostly to uphold the law of retribution: in chapter 15, Eliphaz's description of retribution mentions God only once (v. 25). Bildad's speech in chapter 18 similarly waxes eloquent about the spiritual terrors of the wicked but mentions God only once (v. 21); Zophar's second speech in chapter 20 refers to God only in verses 15, 28–29. This gives the strong impression that the real center of the friends' theology is the retribution principle and the rewards they expect it to bring them. The more the friends talk, the more distant God becomes.

All of this means that an innocent Job is deeply threatening to Eliphaz and his friends. After all, if Job really has remained unstintingly faithful in obedience to God and has suffered so terribly regardless, then the same might happen to them. All their good behavior would turn out to be no defense against unimaginable suffering. On the other hand, if Job is lying about himself and blaming God in order selfishly to hold onto his sin, then all is well.

The world still makes sense, everyone gets what they deserve (in immediate and obvious ways), and Eliphaz and his friends are safe from pain. This is why he goes to such ridiculous lengths to make Job out to be a sinner (22:5–11).

From this perspective, we see that even if Eliphaz's original intention was to comfort Job (2:11), his long condemnations of Job are really an attempt to comfort himself. He never says so, of course. But all his wearying insistence on his narrow version of the principle of retribution is motivated by fear (as Job intuits in 6:21). All of it is intended to reassure himself that Job's suffering will never touch him. In making Job out to be a sinner who is being justly punished, Eliphaz is shoring up his sense of achievement with God and his certainty of being rewarded as a result. He is also shoring up his sense of a coherent, sensible, fair universe where everyone is treated exactly as they deserve.

This is very significant for later readers who want to be wise in how they address Job-like suffering. The book of Job is very canny about human psychology, and especially religious psychology. It was hard for Job's three friends to even look at Job (2:12), and it can be hard for us to talk with our hurting friends as well. It is distressing to see Christian friends suffer and not know why. It can be physically difficult to sit with someone in pain that is overwhelming and that seemingly has no end in sight. Part of the reason for this distress is that we care about our friend. But a larger part of our distress can be a (half-conscious) worry that something similar will happen to us. As a result, it can be extremely tempting, without even realizing it, to blame the sufferer as a way of quarantining ourselves from their agony. Regardless of whether we consciously intend it, blame is a way to reassure ourselves that such suffering will never happen to us, because we are morally superior to the person suffering. This blame can even take theologically sophisticated forms and find Bible verses to quote. We can imply to our Christian friends that they must have made a mistake somewhere along the way, or that God is growing them spiritually. As we saw in the first chapter of this book, these explanations are not always wrong! But when talking to friends who, like Job, freely admit they are not perfect but are genuinely innocent of some terrible secret sin, and who honestly cannot discern any lesson they are supposed to be learning in their ordeal, it can be very enticing to find polite, "biblical" ways to insist that they *do* deserve what they are going through.

This temptation is as subtle as it is persistent. It is so comforting to think we live in a world where terrible suffering will not happen to us because we meet with God's approval. The feeling of personal safety based on a sense of earned righteousness before God is very seductive, and it is unwise to assume we are ever entirely free from it. I remember talking to a very godly Christian friend who had stuck out a bad marriage, but after being cheated on, had gotten divorced. In talking with my friend, I found the thought occurring to me, "Maybe she should have been more alert to early warning signs not to marry this person." But that is just another way to blame the victim—to tell them their pain is (at least in part) their fault. When that thought occurred to me, it was an attempt to comfort myself at the expense of my friend.

In fact, the temptation to be an Eliphaz is so sneaky that it meets people everywhere, whether they are religious or not. Social psychologist Cordelia Fine (herself not a Christian) records her experience of seeing a mother in a park with a severely handicapped baby—and immediately thinking that that mother must not have taken her prenatal vitamins. She recognized the false inference and rejected the idea, but it is significant that the thought occurred to her at all, a trained psychologist, who was sharply aware of this tendency of the human mind. She writes that the "ominous message of this poor woman's loss—'it could be *your* child'—was too distressing to contemplate." But by blaming the victim, we avoid the possibility that it might happen to us and retain our idea of a fair world.[5]

But no matter how sneaky this temptation is, we must constantly guard against it. As we speak to suffering, we must constantly be asking ourselves who we are really trying to comfort: our friend or ourselves. It is very easy to think we are consoling our friend when we are really more interested in our own comfort.

Giving in to this temptation is wrong for the obvious reasons that we will hurt a friend when we could be helping. But this temptation is actually much more dangerous than that. As above, Eliphaz and his pastoral strategy are more horrifying than they first appear. It is worth exploring an Eliphaz-like mentality in its full dimensions, because exposing the full and horrible implications of this particularly persistent way of thinking is no small part of the wisdom of the book of Job.

Blaming innocent sufferers is wrong not just because it hurts them. In the book of Job, victim-blaming is actually a violation of the relational network of love and support God has set up among human beings. Regardless of what we intend or even realize we are doing, condemning an innocent friend forsakes love of neighbor and engages in a kind of sacrifice of our Christian brother or sister for personal benefit—a most un-Christlike attitude. We see this in 6:27, where Job complains that Eliphaz's condemnation of him is tantamount to someone bargaining over human lives like a slave

---

5 Cordelia Fine, *A Mind of Its Own: How Your Brain Distorts and Deceives* (New York: Norton, 2006), 60–61.

trader. This is no exaggeration on Job's part. To point the finger at someone God deeply loves but is allowing to suffer is to relate to him not as an equal but to treat him like property you can use for your own benefit.

But the relational wrongness incurred by blaming an innocent sufferer exists not only horizontally, in our relationship with our Christian brother or sister, but also vertically, in our relationship with God. God has so folded together the relational network with himself and with our neighbor that if we engage in Eliphaz-like condemnation, we are breaking faith with God himself. Job says in 6:14 that someone withholding kindness from a friend "forsakes the fear of the Almighty." As elsewhere in Scripture, our relationships with each other are bound up with our relationship with God. In smearing and discouraging a suffering friend, we incur guilt before God. As we will later see, although God secures their restoration, God is terribly angry with the friends for speaking as they have (42:7–8).

It gets worse. Let's consider what would happen if Job were to give in to the friends—if Job were to invent some sin he knows he has not committed and confess it in order to escape his ordeal. The pressure that the friends put on Job to do so is considerable. More than once, they paint idyllic pictures of the rosy future to which Job can look forward, if only he will admit God was right to let him suffer so terribly (see 5:18–26; 8:5–7, 21; 11:13–19). Imagine what it was like for Job, grieving his children, sick unto death, to have a return to such happiness offered to him. All he has to do is confess he was in the wrong. But consider: if Job caves in to the friends' way of thinking and invents a sin to confess, he is lying to God and compromising integrity with him in order to get his picture-perfect life back—and in so doing, he proves that he values the secondary blessings in a relationship with God more than integrity with God and a right relationship with him. To do so would mean Job falls into the accuser's trap (1:9). As it turns out, although they certainly do not intend it, the friends are actually advancing the accuser's agenda for Job. In the same way, if we pressure a suffering friend to confess a sin where there is none, we may be doing the devil's work for him. May God save us from such cold comforts, such hideous gentleness.

The Ugliness of Moralism

There is one other aspect of Eliphaz's theology that we should notice, again because well-intentioned Christians can imitate it without realizing: its ugliness. As elsewhere, this is not immediately obvious; the friends have a good deal to say about the joyful *shalom* that awaits Job if he will only admit he got what he deserved in chapters 1–2 (see, for example, 5:23–25; 8:21; 11:17). But just as the greatest of distances exists between the surface and depth of the friends' theology, so the true proportion of their counsel is worlds away from real joy and peace.

We get a hint of this in 15:14–16, where, as part of his condemnation of Job as "abominable and corrupt" (v. 16), Eliphaz says the heavens are not clean in God's sight (v. 15). It is only a brief comment, but think about it for a moment. Think about the last time you enjoyed a walk outside in late spring, just as that rich green is blooming everywhere after winter, all under the deep blue of the dome of the heavens and the warm sun. It feels like the whole world wakes up and breathes again after winter. Then think about what an ancient Semite would have associated with uncleanness and abomination—things like bestiality and child sacrifice (Lev. 18:21–25). What kind of internal atmosphere does it take to look at the sky that God has made and say it is ugly, impure, disgusting—like leprosy? And to insist that God sees it that way as well? (We will see later, by the way, in 38:4–7, that God has a very different view of his world.) Jesus said that a good eye means your whole body is full of light (Matt. 6:22), but Eliphaz's neurotic devotion to his narrow version of the retribution principle has so shrunk and twisted his vision that he looks on the most beautiful parts of God's world with disgust, confident all the while that God agrees with him.

Part of wisdom in the Old Testament involved the ability to distinguish appearance from reality and depth from surface. We see this in Proverbs as the son learns to resist sexual entanglements that appear harmless but are actually spiritually deadly (7:13–23), or when he learns that anger is to be met not with more anger but with gentleness (15:1). Part of our pedagogy in the book of Job is learning to discern and appreciate the vast distance between the superficial plausibility of people like Eliphaz and the horrifying implications of their theology. An Eliphaz will have the ability to speak with tact and care and will have some biblical grounding for their assertions. He will also claim to know the way into that deep happiness with God that we all want. But underneath this pleasing appearance is only condemnation and blame, echoing with a kind of cosmic disappointment and disgust with all the good things God has made. This kind of person projects their moralistic frustration with others onto the whole world, and even onto God. To make things worse, it is all spoken from a condescending position of superiority. We have been speaking throughout this book of modern-day Jobs, but it is just as appropriate to speak about modern-day Eliphazes as well. Perhaps you know some. Perhaps you have played the role.

One of the ways we can tell that we have read the book of Job rightly is if we finish the book with a greater caution in how we speak to others—a deeper humility, an unwillingness to assume we understand what God is doing in the midst of suffering, and a deeper hesitancy to blame others. If this set of relational instincts characterizes us to a greater degree by the end of our reading, then the book has met one of its goals. We should still consider further what we *should* say to a modern-day Job, of course. But since we have focused almost exclusively on Eliphaz, and since Job unfortunately has more than one friend speaking to him, let's briefly turn to Job's other friends before sketching what wise and healing words to a modern-day Job might involve.

Cold Comfort: Bildad and Zophar

I mentioned above that the position of the friends in the debate with Job is very simple to summarize. When we look at the speeches of Bildad and Zophar, we see that for all their intense rhetoric and fiery poetry, they have nothing substantially different to say to Job beyond the finger-wagging in which Eliphaz already engaged in chapters 4–5. Bildad takes his first opportunity to speak in chapter 8 to bluntly tell Job that his children got what they deserved (v. 4) but that repentance will make Job's life better than ever (vv. 5–7). Evildoers are quickly done away with (8:13–19), but if Job regains the blamelessness he has forsaken (8:20), Job will be restored (8:21–22; note that v. 22 does come true for Job, but not at all in the way Bildad expects). He spends his second speech waxing eloquent about the spiritual terrors of wicked people (chap. 18) and takes his last turn to speak in chapter 25 to insist that God is so big, everything else looks bad by comparison (the friends repeat a false equation between human smallness and moral fault).

Zophar does no better. In chapter 11, he tells Job that the nightmare of chapters 1–2 is actually gentle treatment from God, and Job deserved much worse (v. 6). Zophar invokes God's transcendent and inscrutable wisdom (11:7–8), but not to comfort Job that his divine friend might be accomplishing far more good than Job could ask or imagine, but only as a bludgeon to put Job in his place and tell him to repent (11:13).[6] His second speech, in chapter 20, has to do with (you guessed it) the punishment of evildoers: no matter how impressive their lives are, they are soon ended (vv. 5–11); no matter how sweet their sin, it only makes them sick (vv. 12–23). Zophar does not speak in the third round (chaps. 22–31). This is an indication that the debate is breaking down and the friends have nothing to left to say to each other. (Thank heaven for small mercies!)

There is not much else to say about the friends. They go on and on and are good poets, but not a single word of theirs is helpful to Job as he agonizes over (what he thinks is) his lost friendship with God and wonders how to get it back. As we drudge our way through these chapters, we do not learn anything new; but they are still part of God's word to us. As we endure their foolish and harmful speech, we grow ever more determined never to imitate them.

Evaluating Elihu

Before we reach the end of the book of Job, however, an angry young man begs a chance to speak. Ancient Israelite wisdom was associated with old age (Job 12:12), so Elihu has waited for the friends to speak first (32:6–7); but now his anger prevents him from being silent. As we will see when we turn to Job's speeches, Job has

---

6 Robert Fyall, *Now My Eyes Have Seen You: Images of Creation and Evil in the Book of Job*, New Studies in Biblical Theology 12 (Downers Grove, IL: InterVarsity Press, 2002), 51.

understandably but wrongly interpreted his situation before God in such a way that either he must be wrong or God must be—and because Job knows he is innocent of any great sin, he is forced to conclude God is in the wrong to punish him. Elihu cannot abide this (32:2). He also cannot stand it that the friends have failed to demolish (what Elihu thinks is) Job's self-justification at God's expense (32:3). Because of this, Elihu promises a new angle on the debate (32:14): he will address Job, so he claims, without invoking the doctrines of the friends.

Does Elihu succeed? People generally take one of two lines when reading the Elihu speeches. On the one hand, some interpret Elihu positively, understanding him not to rebuke Job for some imaginary sin in the past that would explain his present suffering, but to confront the sinful and proud things Job has said against God during the course of the debate. Elihu is thus speaking some hard truths to Job in order to prepare him for his encounter with God. On the other hand, other commentators interpret Elihu as promising a fresh perspective on the debate (32:14) and then failing to deliver as he essentially repeats the ideas of the friends and blames Job. This way of reading Job 32–37 understands these chapters as demonstrating that the human participants in the debate have absolutely no way to resolve Job's problem. They are meant to convince us that God must intervene, or Job will die in despair. Hearing Elihu speak makes us even more anxious for God to speak.

I agree with the second negative interpretation of Elihu because I cannot see what the new insight is that Elihu promises (32:14). He is never able to transcend the suffering-as-punishment idea that the friends have already insisted on at such wearying length. For example, in chapter 33, Elihu confronts Job's complaint that Job wants to meet with God and God is silent (something Job says in

23:3, 8–9). Elihu attacks this by pointing to dreams that prevent pride or some other future sin (33:13–19) or sickness that prompts repentance (vv. 19–22, 26–27). Therefore, it is false to say that God is silent (33:14). So according to Elihu, all of Job's children are dead in one day in order to keep Job from becoming proud, and Job's deadly disease is meant to get him to repent. How is this any different from what the friends have said?

Some readers are impressed with the mediator in 33:23–25, who offers a ransom to save sinners from death. Perhaps there is an anticipation of the Lord Jesus in this passage, similar to Job's hope in a heavenly mediator in 16:18–22 and 19:25–27. But notice how Elihu imagines that this heavenly figure points out people's faults so they can repent (33:23, 26–27), while Job imagines his heavenly friend to act as a witness on his behalf without condemning him. Elihu cannot extricate himself from the idea that Job's suffering is his fault.

Other examples of Elihu's failure to say anything new include his claim that divine silence is explained because no one prays (35:9–11), and when they do, they ask with wrong motives (vv. 12–15). One could also point to his elaboration of divine justice in 36:5–16, according to which God exalts the righteous (v. 7) but takes away their privileges if they sin (vv. 8–9), and calls them to repent (v. 10); if they listen, they are restored (v. 11); otherwise they die in their sin (vv. 12–14). In all that Elihu says, I cannot find anything to which I can imagine Job responding, "Thank you, Elihu. That comforts me and helps me in my pain." His message turns out to be one of condemnation, just as those who spoke before him—and much in contrast to God, who has not a single word of blame for Job when he finally does speak. By the time Elihu finishes, we are more ready than ever to hear him.

How to Speak to Job

Enough of the friends: let's consider what we should say to Job instead of what we should not. As mentioned above, the book of Job does not directly tell us how to address Job-like suffering. But I think we can sketch what a helpful answer would be, if we take an approach exactly opposite from the friends. Our two compass points here are the note of condemnation that rings through almost every line of the friends' speeches and the attitude of self-righteous superiority. In contrast to this, what would it look like to address a suffering friend under the assumption of God's unceasing love and approval (Job 1:8)? And without any assumption of moral superiority to him? That we are just as vulnerable to these inexplicable ordeals as anyone else?

Although doubtless our words will vary from person to person, the following can be helpful to keep in mind.

First, remember that your friend might be so shell-shocked in the early days of his ordeal that he can barely hear you. Lecture him, and all he'll give you is a glassy stare. Remember as well that he is probably receiving "help" from other Christians that is distinctly unhelpful. If your friend does not respond as well as you would like, or does not respond at all, it may be because he is simply unable to.

Asking diagnostic questions about what kind of suffering this is (is there some sin God is bringing to light?) can be helpful, depending on the strength of your relationship, but should only be done slowly and cautiously. The main thing when speaking to a Job is neither to blame nor to suggest God is trying to teach a lesson.

Another helpful thing to remember is that people in pain say crazy things. We will soon see that Job certainly does. When your friend starts saying things about God that are not theologically true, resist the urge to correct him. Your friend's bad theology is only a symptom of a deeper trauma, so addressing the surface issue will do nothing to assuage his deeper pain. Your friend's bad theology is also temporary. As God restores him, God will gently challenge those unworthy things your friend said about his divine friend. God will faithfully be at work to help him see what a perfect Savior he really is (42:5–6). Your job is not to fix your friend but to walk with him.

More positively, tell him no matter how much it might look like it, God's heart is different toward him than he might think. Your friend might feel so hurt that God's love is small comfort, at least at first; but as God is at work in your friend's heart in the midst of his ordeal, the true heart of a Christian will become ever more apparent, which prizes friendship and rightness with God more than anything. Even if he cannot entirely believe it himself, it can be a deep comfort to hear from an outside voice the unchanging reality that God is utterly pleased, happy, and radiantly satisfied with him in Christ and will one day soon prove it by restoring him to fullness and life.

You can also tell your friend that you do not blame him for what he's going through (he may be blaming himself!) and you are not expecting him to learn some lesson. And, odd as it might sound, it can be comforting to tell him that he will need to repeat these truths to you when your own suffering comes.

Perhaps most importantly, tell your friend that you will wait with him until God restores him.

What Have We Learned?

1. Do not blame the sufferer.

2. Just as suffering comes in different kinds, so we need to speak to it in different ways. Sometimes we suffer for our sins and need to be encouraged to repent; sometimes we need en-

couragement to persist in the hard training God is putting us through to grow us.

3. Do not blame.

4. We can speak to friends suffering in Job-like ways with the best of intentions, with pastoral tact, invoking theological ideas that have empirical and scriptural backing, and get it completely wrong in such a way that provokes God's terrible anger at us (Job 42:7–8), tortures someone of whom God is incredibly happy, and advances the devil's agenda for them.

5. You should be very suspicious of yourself—unceasingly so. The temptation to comfort ourselves is so sneaky that we must never stop asking ourselves, when talking with a suffering friend, "The thing I'm about to say—who am I trying to make feel better? My friend or myself?"

6. No blame!

7. It is not until God speaks to Job that Job is satisfied, comforted, and reconciled to God and God's way of running the world. In the same way, God will meet with your brother or sister who is living out Job's story and comfort him or her as only he can. This means your role is not to fix or solve your friends or silence their protests or resolve their trauma. Only God can do that.

8. Resist the temptation to lecture your friends and correct some of the crazy things they say. God will see to that in his own time and gentle way.

9. Find ways to speak to your friends about how God does not hate them (no matter how much it might look like it) and that the ordeal they are going through will not last forever. However nightmarish their lives have become, God *will* restore them. Even if their wounds are so profound that they feel no possible turn of events will ever compensate their losses, God is an expert at restoring permanent tragedy. He has done so with his own Son. However long it takes, he will act. This means that the best thing you can say is, "Let me wait with you for God to restore you."

4

Patiently Listening to Job's Protest and His Faith

(Job 3–37)

I SUGGESTED IN THE LAST CHAPTER that the reason why the author of Job records the friends' speeches at such great length is to frustrate us and prevent us imitating them. A similar sort of question faces us when we turn to Job's speeches and have to work our way through chapter after chapter of agonized protest. Why are we given Job's speeches at such length when his complaint against God's unjust treatment of him could have been much briefer and still faithfully captured what he said? I don't think the narrator is trying to warn us away from imitating Job, as with the friends, because there is plenty of lament and protest elsewhere in the Old Testament. Long sermons of condemnation are never valorized elsewhere in the Old Testament, but lament is a perfectly acceptable form of prayer. On the other hand, Job's words are not recorded for us to make our own in prayer in a simple and direct way, as with psalms of lament. We know this for several reasons. Most importantly, Job himself completely repudiates his past criticisms of God (42:6). The reader's greater knowledge of Job's predicament also prevents us from agreeing with everything Job says in a simple and direct way. Job's speeches are driven by an understandable but completely skewed view of his situation before God and God's heart toward him. God has let Job fall into a situation where Job has every evidence God is against him. This is an essential part of his ordeal, because the results of the test mean nothing if Job knows it is a test. If God had secretly communicated to Job ahead of time what was going to happen and why, the accuser could claim that Job doesn't really love God—he was just saying the right thing without meaning it in order to pass the test and be blessed again in the end.

As a result, Job must remain ignorant throughout his suffering. The sense of inexplicable-ness is essential to a Job-like ordeal. But this means all his attempts to understand his suffering are doomed from the outset; the poor man cannot help but misunderstand what is happening to him and why. So however much we sympathize with Job in his predicament, we listen to his words knowing that he has misread his situation—as Job himself learns by the end (42:6).

Why, then, is Job given eighteen of the book's forty-two chapters to speak, if everything he says is based on the tragically faulty premise that God has betrayed him? I can only conclude that the author wants us to listen to Job without approving of everything he says, but also without blaming or dismissing or rejecting him. We know what the friends say is wrong and so cannot join them in condemning Job. At the same time, we know more of Job's situation than he does, and so we know that not everything Job says is true, for reasons Job cannot even guess. This means that the reader of the book of Job has to sit and listen, without interruption, for a long time, not rejecting Job but also not accepting his own interpretation of his suffering.

Note the effect this has on the reader as well as the profound skill with which the author of Job has put his book together. As we work through this tough book and listen patiently to Job protest, we deepen our ability to listen patiently to the modern-day Jobs we will meet at church. Working through this difficult book is a kind of training in wise and persevering friendship with modern-day sufferers. We become better able to avoid rejecting and condemning them, even when they say some crazy things about God, of which they are later heartily ashamed. As we work through the forty-two chapters of Job, we simultaneously become better able to journey with friends through their ordeals, always keeping in mind the happy resolution God has waiting for them, a resolution our suffering friends can hardly imagine and sometimes hardly even wish for. In other words, the difficulty and wearying length of the book of Job is a crucial part of our training in wisdom. Our journey through the long and frustrating debate deepens our ability to journey with our friends in their Job-like ordeals without falling into the friends' trap of condemning them, while also remembering that the dark things our suffering friends utter in their pain are not the final truth of their lives.

As I speak of "patient listening" with Job, I hope no one thinks I have in mind a clinical detachment from suffering Christian brothers and sisters. On the contrary, the kind of patient and enduring friendship that the book of Job inculcates in us suffers alongside modern-day Jobs, weeping with those who weep (Rom. 12:15), without defending itself against the pain of others. I say this because of the author's choice not to summarize Job's protest with a few brief paragraphs but to record chapter after chapter of intense, complex poetry from Job. The effect of this poetry is to make Job vividly real. Job's poetry is by turns fiery and impassioned, despairing and broken, capable of flights of vision, and at other times quiet and shadowy as the grave itself. If you take your time and let the words percolate, the poetry will go to work on you such that you will taste something of Job's bitterness even if you are not suffering yourself. It is not hard to imagine this great man sitting next to you, at times weeping, at times shouting, at times only able to whisper, at other times caught up in rapturous transport at the thought of somehow reconciling with God. Even though Job's interpretation of his situation is, in the final analysis, wrong—he is very much not suffering under the irrational wrath of God!—the Joban poet wants us to see the world the way Job does. Job's friends sit in the dust near him (2:12–13), but the poet wants us to draw even closer to Job's pain, and it is the poetry that Job utters which allows us to do so. This means that if you feel uncomfortable while reading Job's speeches, that is probably a good sign! The author will not let us interrupt Job with corrections to his wilder claims about God or assurances that everything will end well. There is nothing else to do but journey with this man through his ordeal, taste some of the bitterness, and shiver at a little of the darkness Job sees. As we do, we will be better able to walk with the Jobs we meet in church. Furthermore, we will see a shadowy anticipation of that later Israelite who innocently suffered the wrath of God to rebut the accusations of the devil, and we will better appreciate the fullness of his agony for our sake, of which Job tasted only a little.

Let's come, then, and take our place in the dirt next to a man covered in sores, with empty eyes and a broken voice, and let's listen.

Job's Strange New World (chap. 3)

I stated above my sense that the poet wants us neither to dismiss Job nor imitate him but to journey with him, and that Job's poetry is the means by which the interiority of Job's ordeal is made real to the reader. This is nowhere more evident than in chapter 3, where Job, resigned to the loss of his children, expresses that deeper pain which has so far remained unspoken (2:13) on a canvas as large as creation itself. We are not told explicitly what this deeper pain is, either in the last verse of chapter 2, or in Job's curse in chapter 3; Job's curse on creation in chapter 3 only details what he wants to happen as a result of his pain. But it is not hard to guess. From Job's perspective, God has brought him under a curse, as if Job were a hardened sinner and needed to be punished as such. For no reason Job can think of, his former divine friend is now terribly angry with him and has unleashed the full arsenal of heaven to destroy him. This loss colors everything in Job's universe; every inch of the sky, every itch on Job's festering skin whispers the question, "Why does God hate me when I've given him no reason to?" Even though he does not explicitly articulate this question in chapter 3, it animates every verse.

Job does not curse God in this chapter; he directs a curse against his own existence and (at least by implication) all of creation. But it is a curse that is as vehement as can be. Let the day he was born perish, Job says (v. 3). Let it fall out of every calendar and even God's omniscient reckoning of all of created time (v. 4). As Job adds clause to clause in these verses, the viciousness of his assault on his own existence becomes palpable—not just his birthday, but even the announcement of his conception should be erased (v. 3); let it be reckoned with neither month nor year (v. 6). He even uses the same language in Genesis 1:3 for the creation of light, but with opposite intent, calling for that day to be darkness (Job 3:4).

Sometimes the best way to engage with poetry is not so much to analyze but to immerse oneself in the verbal music and images—to sit with the words and let them linger and percolate. As we sit with 3:3–4, Job's darkness grows ever more total, ever deeper and more sinister. It is a dreadful, deep shadow that Job calls down on himself. He goes so far as to call on the shadow of death in 3:5, the same shadow in which David found comfort in Psalm 23 (but there is no comfort for Job). Even more, Job calls on that deadly shadow to redeem the day of his birth in 3:5. The verb *redeem* here is most often translated as "claim," which is a good translation; since redemption wins rights of ownership, God's redemption of Israel from slavery in Egypt counts as his claim on them. But I wonder if Job means the salvific sense of redeem here. The only salvation Job can see from his new position under God's inexplicable wrath is if he never existed. It is his only redemption from the greatest pain in all his losses: God does not love him.

This is a terrible thing to hear, of course. The text is already preparing us for the sorts of painful things our Christian brothers and sisters will say in their own ordeals. But note that Job's curse is both worse and better than we might at first think. Job is not simply asking to die. This is not the despair of someone saying, "I had a nice life, but everything good in my life is gone, so I wish I was dead." In his memory, Job looks back over the decades of his blessed life and wishes it had never existed in the first place. The happy meals with his wife and children, the orphans he was able to help, the counseling sessions in which he helped wounded sinners back to *shalom* (see 4:3–4)—every moment of it receives Job's curse. As long as Job and God were on good terms, Job was happy to receive every secondary blessing from God. But if God turned on Job for no reason—if Job is now seeing a side to God he never suspected but was lurking there all along—if all Job's happy past was a sinister means by which God could set Job up for disaster (as Job says in 10:8–13)—then Job is not interested in the charmed life he used to enjoy. None of the secondary blessings that accrue to obedience interest Job in the slightest without right standing before God. Without the friendship of God, Job wants none of it. It is hard to hear Job utter a curse against the whole of his existence, but his motives are noble. Strange as it might sound, Job's curse on the day of his birth actually expresses the same high view of God as in 1:21, only in a negative way. Furthermore, Job is right to value intimacy with God more than a blessed life. The only thing he is wrong about is how God really views him.

Hopefully by now we can appreciate the true magnitude of Job's nightmare that drives his curse and his dismaying desire for redemption in the grave. How terrible even the best and happiest of lives become without the friendship of God! Why, why did Job ever leave the womb, if it meant he would have to see the day when God's hatred of him was finally revealed (3:9–10)? If Job had been stillborn (3:11), he could have found peace of a sort in Sheol, far away from that angry God (3:13). Job knows that all earthly distinctions are erased in the diminished and shadowy existence that all the shades in Sheol have—whether small or great, all alike persist in a kind of interminable nonentity (3:19). This means everything distinctive about Job's life would be erased as well—especially the day he learned who God really was. He would be safe from God's inexplicable wrath and delivered from the false happiness of his old life. So it is there that Job's thoughts turn, his longing expressed in the repeated "There. . . . There. . . .

There . . ." in verses 17–19. The dreary, dim existence of those poor souls in Sheol is far preferable to Job than his present broken relationship with God.

Job's first poem is hard to read. The intensity of Job's curse lingers after we finish the chapter, and the reader's knowledge that God's heart toward him is actually unchanged, and that God has a wonderful conclusion to Job's story waiting for him, does nothing to dispel the dismay his poetry evokes. This chapter is preparing us for the dismaying things our own friends will say when they suffer. It is also helping us appreciate how the world looks through their eyes. But this is only Job's first chapter. We need to brace ourselves: Job's mind has not yet started to explore the full dimensions of the strange new world into which his suffering has initiated him. Although some truly remarkable statements of faith await us, Job is taking only his first steps into the abyss.

Job's Protest against God (chaps. 6–7; 9–10)

We have already mentioned parts of Job's speech in chapter 6 and the way he responds to Eliphaz's well-intentioned but blundering help. The main thing Job insists on in this chapter is that his suffering is due to a vicious and irrational attack from God (6:4; cf. 16:9–17) and does not represent measured, fair punishment for secret sin, as Eliphaz claimed. He also rails against Eliphaz for failing to say anything helpful or healing to him (6:15–27). Comparing wise speech to water (just as Proverbs does in 10:11; 15:4), Job says he is as disappointed with his friends as a thirsty man in the desert who needs water and finds only a dry riverbed (6:15–20).

But it is not really the friends that Job is interested in. In chapter 7, he turns to consider his new position before God and desperately tries to find some perspective by which he could explain why God turned on him. Is Job some kind of cosmic threat to God, requiring the full weaponry of heaven to come crashing down on him (7:12)? (The sea is an important symbol for cosmic chaos in the Old Testament, and it will be an important image to remember when we come to God's speeches.) Why would God (as it were) put so small a creature as Job under such microscopic scrutiny (7:17–18)? And if there were some sin in Job that could somehow explain why God was so terribly provoked against him, is that really such a profound threat that God has to decimate Job's life so thoroughly (7:20)? And why is forgiveness for this hypothetical sin suddenly off the table, especially when so many past sins were already forgiven (7:21)?

From Job's limited perspective, there were only two people involved in chapters 1–2: God and himself. Job is testing hypotheses that would explain (what looks like) the punishment of chapters 1–2 in relation to himself and coming up empty. In his next speech, in chapters 9–10, he will try to explain his suffering in relation to God. Job will (not without horror) think through the possibility that God is punishing him because God is not a good and fair person. As he does so, Job will sink to his low point.

Job signals the trajectory of chapters 9–10 in the second verse: "How can a man be in the right before God?" (9:2). Job is responding to Bildad's speech in chapter 8 with this question, but it must have been frustrating for Bildad to hear, because he just answered it for Job: repent (8:5). But Job knows (as does the reader) that he has done nothing of which he needs to repent. So when he asks the question of 9:2, he is wondering out loud how he could prove to God that he did not deserve (what looks like) the punishment of chapters 1–2. As this chapter proceeds, a new and terrible thought dawns on Job: if Job could somehow summon God to court, and if it were somehow possible to find some kind of tribunal that could try his case, the judge would decide in Job's favor and prove God to be in the wrong.

This is a terrible thing to say, of course, but it is helpful to keep in mind two aspects of this speech that provide just an edge of a silver lining. The first is that Job's deepest desire is to be right with God. Even if he states this desire in a distorted or foolish way, it is still very admirable that the one loss that pains Job most deeply out of all his losses is the loss of intimacy with God.[1] In fact, we will see throughout Job's speeches that he only and obsessively talks about God and how to be right with God again; not a single time does he ever ask for his blessed life back.

The second hopeful aspect of this chapter is that Job can barely utter the idea of winning a court case against the Almighty before Job's admirable sense of God's awesome transcendence and greatness drowns it out. In 9:3, Job readily admits that if he were to enter into litigation with the Almighty, he would not be able to answer a single question under cross-examination (the image here is of two parties arguing their case before a judge). Even though Job knows he is right, he would be so overwhelmed by God that his own mouth would trip him up (9:20), and he, the wronged party, would be reduced to begging his legal opponent for mercy (9:15). How could he even serve the almighty sovereign of the universe with a court summons or believe that God was even listening to a dust speck like himself (9:16)? Dreadful as this chapter is, Job is not arrogantly and casually railing against a God before whom he has never trembled. This is a terrible matter for Job, one he feels himself forced into by his inexplicable predicament.

---

1   Christopher Ash, *Job: The Wisdom of the Cross*, Preaching the Word (Wheaton, IL: Crossway, 2014), 141.

Despite these hopeful glimmers, chapter 9 is nevertheless Job's absolute low point in the debate, in which he utters his darkest suspicions about God. One the one hand, Job *knows* there is no secret pattern of sin that could explain God turning the principle of retribution against him and putting Job in the "sinner" category. This pushes Job to conclude that God must not be good, something that any impartial third party would recognize. On the other hand, it is the almighty Lord with whom Job has to deal. Who could ever score points against the all-knowing, infinite Creator in a debate? How could you even utter a single syllable in his presence? Especially one as given to such violent outbursts as seen in chapters 1–2 (see also 9:17)! Again, Job does not know about the larger canvas of which we read in chapters 1–2. He does not know about the accuser's question and God's deeper purpose in allowing Job's trauma. His limited perspective positions him so that Job finds it impossible not to draw some terrifying new conclusions about God.

He speaks these conclusions in 9:22–24, a short passage that represents a kind of summary of his case against God's injustice and one of the hardest passages to read in the entire book. "It is all one," Job says (9:22). It does not matter if you are faithful to God and demonstrate integrity with him; he will destroy your life eventually. (Notice how Job is extrapolating outward from his limited perspective on his tragedy in chapters 1–2 to draw sweeping conclusions about God and his administration of all creation.) Even worse, God thinks it is funny when innocent lives fall apart (9:23). In fact, God himself deliberately frustrates the execution of justice in the human realm; by covering the faces of judges, God prevents them from securing justice for the helpless (9:24). As a result, the worst sort of people get to run everything (9:24). Job will repeat this protest against divine injustice elsewhere in his speeches (see 12:13–25; 19:5–12; 21:7–33; 24:1), but he states it most sharply here. If it is not God doing this, Job asks, then who else could it be (9:24)? And it is just at this point that our sympathy with Job is highest, while we also want to distance ourselves from his conclusion most sharply, for although Job's limited perspective makes his question inevitable, we know he is getting God exactly wrong. There are more parties involved in heaven and earth than Job knows, and God actually cares deeply for justice and for Job himself, as Job will learn when God finally speaks.

But just as it is not always wise or helpful to interrupt and correct our friends who say crazy things in their pain, we must keep listening to Job as he laments his quickly fading existence (9:25–26; 10:18–22) under God's inexplicable verdict of guilty (9:27–10:4; 10:14–17; Job arranges the parts of his speech in a chiasm, with 10:8–13 as the climactic midpoint). Even here, Job is turning his predicament over and over in his mind, trying to find some kind of resolution. He honestly wants to know why God is condemning him like a flagrant evildoer (10:2). Why would God (as it were) put Job on the rack and try to torture a confession out of him when his omniscient Creator already knows he will find no sin in Job (10:4–7)? Job cannot explain his tragedy in relation to himself. His only recourse is to explain it in relation to God and to reinterpret his past life of blessing (10:8–12) as a sinister way for a master torturer to get Job relaxed and comfortable, just so he could pounce on him when Job least suspects it (10:13). God set him up.

Job does not hold back in any of his speeches (see 16:6), and the Joban poet does not censor or mute or "pretty up" any of Job's criticisms of God. As we see the world from Job's very gloomy perspective, the reader is better able to appreciate how some modern-day Jobs will feel and better able to sympathize with them. Fortunately,

Job will not stay at this low point forever. But before turning to some of the remarkable statements of faith that Job makes in the ordeal, let's consider two more oddly hopeful notes in this very gloomy point in Job's journey.

First, Job's personal integrity even in the midst of his ordeal is very striking. In 10:15, Job actually calls down a curse on his own head if he has sinned (the phrase "woe to me" in this verse is a kind of self-imprecation). Job does not use God's apparent betrayal of him as an excuse to indulge his favorite sins (see 27:5–6). He maintains his obedience to God in good times and bad, even when it appears that obeying God is pointless. In fact, since the losses of chapters 1–2 would have counted as curses for disobedience within the theological framework of Job and his friends, Job's self-imprecation in 10:15 amounts to agreeing that God would have been right to curse him, if Job had engaged in secret sin. In other words, Job's sense of being attacked and wounded by God does not mean he tries to strike back. He does not surrender personal integrity before God even in the midst of extreme suffering.

A second hopeful note in chapters 9–10 is easy to miss but quite profound. In 9:21, Job says that he has no regard for his own life. This is a good translation of the Hebrew and makes sense in context as Job both sinks under a sense of smallness before God and feels only loathing for the life he has been given. One could, however, translate this phrase more literally as "I do not know myself" (the verb *yāda'* can be translated either as "know" or "have regard for"). To my mind, this is significant. It is as if Job, suffering under a broken relationship with God and bereft of his friendship, has simultaneously lost his grip on his own self. On the one hand, he knows he is blameless (9:21)—he *knows* he has done nothing to deserve (what looks like) the punishment of chapters 1–2. But when Job turns his mind to God, all his certainty is dwarfed before infinity. No matter how deep Job's sense of his own blamelessness in this ordeal might be, it cannot make a claim on God. As a result, Job cannot know for certain what he knows about himself (Paul says exactly the same in Galatians 4:9 and 1 Corinthians 8:2–3). Job knows he cannot autonomously make a claim to righteousness on his own; he needs God to vindicate him and show him to be in the right. Just as in chapter 3, this is actually quite good theology! Job is wrong only about God's heart toward him.

The reader's larger perspective on Job's predicament means we can interpret some of the things he says in something of a positive way. For no fault of his own, however, Job cannot. He ends his speech wondering why God made him at all (10:18). Job's best-case scenario is that his divine torturer will simply leave off and ignore him for a few days (10:20), before Job enters that profound darkness that is the end of all mankind (10:21–22). Job here has reverted to the despair of chapter 3. His darkness is chilling in its finality.

Job's Emerging Hope of Reconciliation with God (chaps. 12–14; 16–17; 19; 23)

In mentioning some hopeful elements in Job's protest against God, I left out what might be the most hopeful aspect of Job's protest but perhaps the most difficult to see: no matter how he rails against God, Job does not curse him. Despite the terribly dark and suspicious things Job says, he does not cut off his relationship with God and walk away. However slight the difference is between saying, "God is not good, does not care about right behavior, and runs his world in an unjust way," and saying, "I want nothing more to do with this God," Job will affirm the former but not the latter. This is already encouraging—Job's ordeal has not destroyed his faith! But

Job's refusal to curse becomes even more striking when we consider that Job's protest has provided him with some compelling reasons to give up on God. After all, if everything Job says in 9:22–24 is true, why would you not break a relationship with that kind of deity? Job portrays God in that passage as if he were one of those horrible dictators we read about in the news, laughing and happy in his palace while innocent people rot in prison camps. Surely it would be morally wrong to remain a loyal, faithful subject of a dictator like that? And yet even when Job paints himself into a corner and says things about God that might make us certain that he will curse God and die, Job cannot bring himself to do so. In fact, in a surprising and beautiful way, despite the terrible things Job says, and without surrendering his claim against God, Job begins to long for reconciliation with God and will spend more and more time in his later speeches imagining what a reunion with his long-lost divine friend might look like.

We see this first in chapter 13. Like a single flower rising out of dry ground, Job briefly and tentatively wonders if he and God could somehow sit down together and talk things out (13:13–23). It does not matter to Job who speaks first (13:23); Job is happy to listen and respond, or Job can begin and then listen to what God has to say. If there is some fault in Job that could explain (what looks like) God's terrible anger and the punishment of chapters 1–2, Job says in 13:24 that he genuinely wants to know and is happy to repent, if only it means he and God could be friends again. Once again, do not miss Job's integrity in his ordeal: he is exposing himself to the possibility of further judgment from God in this verse, but his desire to enjoy once again God's friendship compels him. Despite the criticisms Job has leveled against God (of which he is later heartily ashamed), Job's deepest desire is to be right with God, and his deepest agony among all his losses is the thought that God has rejected him.

This potential sit-down with the Almighty is, however, a terrifying matter for Job (13:13–14). The nightmare of chapters 1–2 makes it impossible for Job to feel entirely safe around God; he feels the need to request ahead of time that this inscrutable deity not so totally overwhelm him that Job cannot even speak (13:20–21). It is difficult to hear Job express this fear (imagine listening to a Christian friend describe God as an abusive parent). But note again how strong, how admirable Job's desire to reconcile with God must be in order to take (what he thinks is) such a risk. Despite what it might cost him, there is an impulse within Job to meet with God that simply will not die: "Though he slay me, I will hope in him" (13:15). Job 13:15 is a famous verse, and justly so; but it is easy to miss the full dimensions of Job's hope. Since death is the final divine judgment for sin, Job is saying in verse 15 that God can treat him even worse than he already has, and Job will continue to trust in God regardless. When we remember that Job credits God as the immediate source of his losses in chapters 1–2, we can appreciate how moving a confession this is. The mere fact that Job would desire reconciliation at all is surprising; that he would continue to trust God even if God deepens Job's nightmare is amazing. Job wants relational rightness before God so deeply that he will risk further disaster to get it.

Job does finish 13:15 by saying he'll continue to argue and protest directly to God's face. Job's limited perspective on his tragedy means he thinks of God as his adversary, who turned on him for no reason. Job also persists in his conviction that any objective third party would agree that God mistreated Job (13:18). Job will absolutely reject his case against God by the end of the book and realize how wrong he was to portray God as unjust and uncaring (42:5–6), but for now, his hope for reconciliation with God exists simultaneously with his conviction that he has been wronged by God. This generates several contradictions, one of which we noticed above (i.e., if God is really as bad as Job has said, one wonders why Job would even want to reconcile with such an ominous, threatening deity).

Another contradictory aspect to Job's simultaneous protest and faith is the way that Job insists both that personal integrity means nothing to God (as in 9:22–24) and that his personal integrity means he will get a fair hearing with God (13:16). This contradiction will persist in Job's speeches. He will insist both that God cares nothing for treating good people well and that God cares enough about obedience that if he and Job could just meet, God would recognize that Job has done nothing worthy of such terrible punishment, vindicate him, and God and Job could be friends again (23:3–7). Job's protest excludes any room for hope in God, and his hope unsettles the dark certainties of his protest. The two contradict each other, but Job maintains both.

In pointing to the contradictions in Job's speeches, I am not at all criticizing him. I am trying to show how striking his faith is, how seemingly impossible to explain. No matter how much of a beating Job's faith takes, no matter how much he suffers, even when Job gives himself every reason to give up on God, his hope simply will not die. In fact, Job finishes chapter 17 by saying that his hope prevents him from embracing death (vv. 13–16). We should remember when we read this that the desire for death dominates Job's first three speeches (3:11–23; 7:21; 10:20–22). As he continues to speak, however, Job finds a hope within himself that will not let him settle down as a shade in Sheol, with his relationship with God forever broken. The change in Job from his first speech to the end of chapter 17 is as admirable as it is moving. Even though the text does not explicitly tell us, I hardly know how to explain Job's growing hope outside of the preserving work of the Holy Spirit.

Chapter 13 is the first appearance of Job's hope in God in the midst of his protest, but it disappears quickly; Job no sooner states his desire to meet with God (v. 22) than he is again overwhelmed by what he perceives to be God's overwhelming anger toward him (vv. 24–27). By the chapter's final verse, Job's hope has apparently disappeared, and all he can see is humanity worn out and wiped away by divine anger (13:28). He spends all of the next chapter under these unbroken storm clouds; while some parts of nature might enjoy renewal (14:7–9), humanity is denied this blessing and instead wilts quickly under God's harsh treatment (14:1–6, 18–22). The whole chapter is dominated by images of the world dissolving, losing its consistency, being worn away—mountains crumble, water rubs stones smooth, rain washes away soil (14:18–19). But just as Job is apparently unable to maintain even the meager crest of hope that rises in chapter 13, he is equally unable to remain in the gloom of chapter 14. We see this in chapters 16 and 19.

These two chapters contain two justly famous passages in which Job describes his heavenly mediator. It is as if the thought of possible renewal before God's presence (even resurrection) from 14:7, 14 blossoms in his mind, and what he denied in chapter 14 comes to grip him with deeper certainty. Both of these hopeful passages continue the contradictory aspect of Job's hopeful protest and protesting hope. We can see this in the way that both are preceded by vicious denunciations of God's unjust treatment of him: in 16:7–17, the violence of God's unprovoked attack on Job takes on an almost dizzying ferocity; in chapter 19, God has ambushed and so decimated Job (vv. 7–12) that not a single other human being will even get close to him, and everyone treats him like a stranger (vv. 13–19). Both mediator passages are also grounded in Job's expectation of soon-approaching death (16:18, 22; 19:23–24).

Job thinks he will very soon die, with his case unresolved and his relationship with God still unhealed—but Job also hopes his mediator will work on his behalf and somehow end the breach between himself and God. Another similarity between these passages is that Job expresses an absolute certainty about his mediator in both. In 16:19, Job says there is someone testifying on his behalf "even now, behold," as if his heavenly friend is speaking even as Job speaks. In 19:25, Job goes so far as to say that he *knows* his Redeemer lives. Job does not explain why he is so certain, and perhaps he does not fully understand it himself. It is as if Job's hope for reconciliation with God is gripping him ever more deeply, so much so that he cannot help but rejoice in the heavenly friend working on his behalf even now.

This is Job's great hope: that his mediator will repair the relationship between God and himself and bring the two of them together so that Job's deepest desire can be fulfilled and he can live under God's smile again. This is clear from 16:19, 21 but is also present in the exact wording of 19:25, even though it is harder to see in English translation. Job speaks in 19:25 of a kinsman-redeemer, a social role in ancient Israel by which one could help a disadvantaged relative by buying back land sold under financial distress or by buying a relative back from slavery (see Lev. 25:25–28, 35–46; Ruth 4:1–12). A kinsman-redeemer could also engage in legal argument on behalf of someone accused (Ps. 119:154; Prov. 23:11; Jer. 50:34; Lam. 3:58–59). It is this aspect of the kinsman-redeemer's work in particular that Job has in mind in 19:25. Part of Job's torment is that he feels falsely accused by God—the apparent punishment of chapters 1–2 feels to Job like an accusation of guilt from on high. But when Job says his Redeemer will "stand," he uses a word elsewhere describing a witness who rises in court to offer testimony (see Deut. 19:15–16; Job 16:8; Pss. 27:12; 35:11).[2] This means that Job hopes his Redeemer's testimony will melt God's angry accusations against Job so that they can be friends again. Because of his Redeemer, Job will see God and not a stranger (19:27), healing Job's present isolation and alienation (19:13, 15).[3]

The way Job describes his Redeemer's work in 19:25–27 goes beyond legal representation, however. Although it is not easy to see even in a good translation, Job poetically communicates at multiple levels to speak in this passage of a cosmic act of redemption from the grave, in addition to a legal witness. We are rightly familiar with how Job's Redeemer will "stand upon the earth" (as a witness on Job's behalf). But Job literally says that his Redeemer will "rise above the dust" or "triumph over" it. To translate this verse as "stand upon the earth" is not misleading, since that verb is used elsewhere for offering legal testimony, and "dust" can stand for the ground or the world more generally (see, e.g., Job 14:8, 19; 28:2). But dust is also a symbol for death and the grave in the book of Job (see 7:21; 17:16; 20:11, 26; 34:15; 40:13). Furthermore, the verb that Job uses, although occasionally correctly translated as "stand," more often should be translated as "rise above" or "triumph over."[4] More than once, it expresses God's action of self-exaltation to save his

---

2 John Hartley, *The Book of Job*, New International Commentary on the Old Testament (Grand Rapids, MI: Eerdmans, 1988), 294.

3 19:27 is usually translated as Job seeing God "and not another," which is a good translation, but Job literally says he will see God "and not a stranger," echoing his use of this root in vv. 13, 15 and reversing his present loneliness.

4 The verb used in Job 19:25 is *qûm*, "to rise up." Normally, "to stand" is expressed by the verb *'āmad*.

helpless people (see Pss. 3:8; 7:7; 9:22; 10:12; 12:6; 44:27; 68:2; 74:22; 76:10; 82:8).

This means that when we hear of Job's Redeemer standing on the earth as a legal advocate, we should simultaneously hear Job confessing his hope that his Redeemer will "rise above the dust" in the sense of triumphing over death.[5] Remember that death is very much on Job's mind; he is very sick (2:7), and death is the final penalty for sin, the final consequence of the divine judgment that Job thinks he is suffering. Just as Job feels himself slipping toward the grave under God's inexplicable wrath, however, his hope somehow grows ever brighter. In addition to offering testimony about Job's integrity to God, Job now expresses his hope that his Redeemer will save him fully and totally from all the effects of God's anger, even death itself. This is the ultimate way in which Job's mediator can bring Job and God together again in friendship. Awareness of the multiple meanings in 19:25 also helps us appreciate Job's statement that his Redeemer "lives." It is out of the power of his own indestructible life that Job's Redeemer triumphs over death to Job's benefit.

The result of his Redeemer's triumph is detailed in 19:26–27: after he dies, Job will be joyously reunited with God. Job's skin being destroyed is a poetic way of referring to his death ("skin" stands for Job's body in 2:4; 7:5). Furthermore, seeing God in 19:26–27 means more than some distant glimpse; it means being caught up in God himself as Job is reunited in fellowship with him. The verb Job uses is found elsewhere in the Old Testament for prophetic visions of

---

5   It is worth mentioning that more than once in the book of Job, characters will describe death as "lying down" in the dust—the opposite verb "rising" from the dust (see 7:21; 20:11; 21:26). Furthermore, in 14:12, Job uses the verb *qûm* to say he will not rise from death (the same phrase recurs in Isa. 26:19 as a way of describing the resurrection). This strengthens the likelihood that Job's Redeemer "rising above the dust" is an OT way of speaking about resurrection hope.

the divine (Ex. 24:11; Num. 24:4, 16; Isa. 30:10) or in the Psalms for deep intimacy with God (Pss. 11:7; 17:15; 27:4; 63:3). Job is here expressing the same rapturous hope that Christians feel when they read about seeing Jesus's face in Revelation 22:4. This means that the happiest of reunions awaits Job after death, all because of his Redeemer's triumph. Someday that loss that pained Job most deeply in all his suffering will finally be restored, and he will be embraced in fellowship by God. Note as well how this is no vague, ghostly existence, like the shades in Sheol; when Job refers to his flesh (19:26) and his own eyes (19:27), he is speaking of embodied existence in God's presence after death. Although the hope of the resurrection is fully and clearly revealed only in the New Testament, it is hard for me to see how Job's hope here is any different. What a profound confession this is from an Old Testament saint!

It was profound for Job as well. Do you see how Job lingers over the thought of seeing God and not a stranger? Three times in 19:26–27, Job speaks of seeing God, as if captivated by the thought. Somehow, somehow, Job *knows* that he has a mighty divine friend and Redeemer who is working on his behalf. Job is confident he will be raised to new life and favor in God's presence, and all of his tragedy (and the incomprehensible divine anger that Job thinks caused it) will be only a bad dream he can hardly remember. Not even the grave itself will be able to separate God and Job. No matter how deeply Job feels wounded by God, he cannot suppress the hope of being with him again. Somehow, somehow, "all shall be well, and all shall be well, and all manner of thing shall be well."[6]

Job is, of course, speaking better than he knows here—everything he says is true, but in a happier way than he can imagine. Job feels

---

6 Julian of Norwich, *A Lesson of Love: The Revelations of Julian of Norwich*, ed. Father John-Julian OJN (London: Darton, Longman & Todd, n.d.), 61.

so wounded by God that he cannot picture his heavenly Father acting as a redeemer for him and so imagines a separate mediator speaking on his behalf to an angry judge. The modern-day Jobs you meet will probably say similar things. Job will learn, however, that God's heart toward him is entirely different from what he fears. He will learn who his heavenly Redeemer really is, that he is more closely and immediately at work than Job ever dared imagine, and that he need not wait until after his death to see God. God has similar mercies waiting for modern-day Jobs who cannot bring themselves fully to trust the God who allowed such terrible pain into their lives but also cannot suppress their hope that somehow, somehow, all will be well.

Job's Final Words (chaps. 29–31)

I mentioned above how Job's hope exists simultaneously (and contradictorily) with Job's protest against God. Job never retreats from the hope of chapter 19, but he also continues to insist that (what looks like) his punishment from God was totally undeserved. This dominates his last speech, in which he looks back longingly over his past blessed life (chap. 29), laments his present misery (chap. 30), and swears to his own innocence (chap. 31). Chapter 31 is significant because Job engages in a self-imprecation that, in an Old Testament framework, God is expected to respond to by either denying or upholding it. This chapter is tantamount to someone saying, "May God damn me if I committed this sin." In other words, if God remains silent, it is assumed that the person making the oath is innocent. Job is forcing the issue: God must respond to Job's oath, or Job's protest against God's injustice will appear to be vindicated.

It is important to remember that it is Job's desire for relational rightness with God that drives the self-imprecation of chapter 31 (see v. 6, "Let God know my integrity!"). In fact, the first loss Job mentions in chapter 29 is his lost friendship with God (vv. 2–4). Furthermore, the long description of his blessed prior life is not an indirect way of asking for any of his blessings to be given back but only enlisted as part of a larger argument about his own innocence and undeserved suffering. It undergirds the claim, "Let God know my integrity!" Despite this, however, a feeling of unease lingers as Job finishes speaking (31:40). Job has articulated a future encounter between himself and God such that one party will be shown to be in the wrong and the other justified: either God stays silent and tacitly admits an innocent man was punished in a terrible travesty, or God somehow proves Job wrong. Fortunately, when God does finally appear, he directly addresses Job's complaint without letting himself be entangled in the false dilemma Job has constructed. But even though Job's desire for rightness with God is admirable, one feels a little uneasy as Job's final speech ends. Job cannot see how he can suffer innocently and God can be good at the same time. In fact, although I argued above that Elihu doesn't have anything helpful to say to Job, I wonder if part of the reason his speeches were included is to prevent any idea that Job summoned God. God does respond in faithfulness to Job, but not because Job "forced" him to.

At this point in the book, the debate between Job and his friends has totally exhausted itself. On the one hand, the friends have failed catastrophically to help Job in the slightest. On the other hand, although Job has expressed remarkable faith in God and an amazing hope for reconciliation, this faith cannot resolve his terrible sense that God has wronged him—and if he has, what does that say about God? Job cannot resolve this problem.

It is time for the Lord to speak.

Seeing a Job-Like Ordeal from the Inside

I have argued in this chapter that Job's speeches are preserved in order to help us be better friends and fellow travelers with modern-day Jobs. Job's poetry does this by vividly communicating for the reader how the world and the God ruling it look from the inside of a Job-like ordeal. The picture that emerges is staggering. We have seen in chapter 3 how Job's nightmare contaminates every moment of his blessed past; if he and God are not on good terms, if Job now knows the sinister truth about God's real character (see 10:8–13), then Job cannot be at peace with a single moment of his existence, no matter how happy. Nor is there anything in the future Job can look forward to (7:7); even if his formerly blessed life were to magically return, how could Job enjoy any of it without God's friendship?

Deepening the bizarre, Kafkaesque proportions of Job's nightmare is that Job knows he has done nothing to deserve the angry punishment he's receiving from God. And surely the omniscient Creator must know it as well (10:4–7)? What, then, could possibly have caused this terrible change in his divine friend? What sort of person would treat an imperfect but sincere saint like Job so brutally? Is Job's entire existence some kind of sick joke (10:18)? A way for God to slowly pull the wings off a fly, as the fly whimpers and moans about how he thought they were friends?

Another angle by which we can appreciate the depth of Job's nightmare is (strange as it might sound) to trace how little his theology changes because of his suffering. Job still believes in God's absolute sovereignty and power (9:3–19). He even still credits God with wisdom (12:13)—"wisdom" here meaning something like "effective ability" (see, e.g., Ex. 28:3; 31:3, 6; Eccles. 2:3, 9). Job sees God's wisdom expressed in the great skill by which God distorts the moral order of the world (see Job 12:13–25). The only change in Job's theology has to do with God's goodness: Job thinks he has compelling evidence that he cannot really trust God anymore. But imagine an all-knowing, all-powerful being who was not a good and trustworthy person. Imagine what it would feel like, sitting on the ash heap, under the gaze of such a terrible God, when you had worked so hard to serve that God and care for the widow and orphan, as false friends preach at you from the safety of their own comfortable lives about how you deserve everything you are going through. Imagine how this new view of God would overshadow every moment of your existence.

The more we appreciate the depth of Job's nightmare, the more we admire his steadfastness in his ordeal (see James 5:11), and even more so his desire to reconcile with the God who wounded him so deeply. It is impossible not to feel pity for him as well, for Job would not agonize so violently about his lost friendship with God if he did not love God so profoundly. And all the while, Job has no idea of the true state of God's heart toward him (1:8).

I stated above that part of the reason for the vivid poetry of Job's speeches is to communicate what a Job-like ordeal feels like from the inside. The God who inspired this book, however, has a far more intimate relation to Job-like ordeals than any human reader has, for God has undergone Job's agony himself in the person of his Son. I hinted already at the way in which Job anticipates Jesus. This connection is not made explicitly in the New Testament, but I find it impossible to avoid: as we see Job sitting on the ash heap, stricken and grieving and suffering innocently what looks like the unrestrained fury of God for sin, who can fail but to think of the greater sufferings of the only perfectly innocent man who ever lived? Who, though perfect, underwent many hells in bearing the wrath of God for many millions on the cross, all to seal us in a Job-like relationship with God, where he is loved and cherished sincerely and for his own sake, irrespective of what we gain or lose along the way? In the person of his Son, God knows fully and intimately the agony of every Job (ancient or modern), because he drank to the dregs that cup of which Job was given only a sip. Whenever God allows one of his children to suffer a Job-like ordeal, it is but a whisper, the barest hint of the suffering that his Son lovingly bore for our sake.

This means that if we as readers find the vivid poetic representation of Job's ordeal staggering—if the mixture of Job's protest and his faith burst all bounds of proportion—then words will hardly suffice to express the suffering of that greater Job and the faithfulness he evidenced throughout. How can this fail to humble us as Christians? Doesn't the fact that Jesus entered into Job's predicament and suffered more than Job make you love Jesus more? Doesn't a determination to serve our greater Job rise in your heart as you consider how Job is only an anticipation of Jesus—even while knowing that Job-like ordeals will sometimes be ours?

All of this is to say that as the Joban poet presents Job's ordeal to us ever more vividly, we see Christ prefigured—and, to a lesser extent, we can recognize our own story. But our Job-like ordeals, serious as they are, are swallowed up before the view of the vaster agony of God the Son.

Happily, Christ now reigns at the right hand of the Father, never to taste the bitterness of death again. God also has a wonderful happy ending waiting for Job that Job cannot presently imagine. The book of Job does not quickly take us to God's speeches and Job's restoration, however. Part of our training in wisdom in this book is to sit with Job in the dust, listen, see Jesus prefigured, understand better the modern-day Jobs we meet, and recognize that a Job-like ordeal is one chapter in our life of discipleship.

What Have We Learned?

1. Your Christian friends undergoing Job-like ordeals will say terribly troubling things about God. The sense of God's untrustworthiness is part of their ordeal. They will simultaneously express (helped by the Spirit) profound hope in God (13:15). Part of a Job-like ordeal is getting to the end of your rope and finding that you trust God more than you ever thought you could. Your friends will not be able to resolve this contradiction, and you should not try to. Encourage them in their faith, remembering that the same impossible happy ending that God had waiting for Job will be given to each saint who, empowered by the Spirit, trusts God to the end.

2. God will sometimes allow his saints to fall into a position where it looks as if he has completely given up on them and does not love them anymore. This is only an appearance; God's heart is (if I can put it this way) unchangingly, unstintingly proud of his children (1:8). But a major part of the wisdom of the book of Job is to warn us ahead of time that there will be times when we find ourselves asking, "What concrete evidence do I have that God actually loves me? I treat my own children better than God treats me." Just as the speeches of Job's friends teach us to be suspicious about our tendency to blame, so Job's speeches prevent us from making quick assumptions about God's heart toward us in suffering. There is

so much we do not understand, so many factors impinging on our lives that we cannot grasp.

3. A Job-like ordeal has a peculiar dignity to it: God has entrusted his reputation to Job and every later saint who suffers like him.

4. In suffering, God can feel inaccessible, as if he is not listening (23:8–9). It is not true—but even when you find it difficult to believe that God loves you and attends to every word you say, you have the Son of God speaking on your behalf, who is far closer to God than you, who knows suffering more intimately than you do.

5. Whether we are suffering a Job-like ordeal or not, Job's speeches should give us greater sympathy with those who are and a deeper love and awe for the Lord Jesus, whose sufferings are only prefigured in Job's nightmare.

6. The book of Job goes on for a long time. There simply is no quick or easy resolution to suffering. God is always faithful to meet with and restore his saints who persevere in trusting him, but not quickly.

5

Job's Limits, God's Goodness, and the Continuing Presence of Evil

(Job 38:1–40:5)

EVERY TIME I READ the book of Job, I begin chapter 38 with a sigh of relief: finally, God will rebuke the friends, comfort Job, and set everything right! A quick reading of God's speeches can leave the reader more confused than reassured, however, because God seems to talk about everything in the universe except what we expect him to. God takes Job on a tour of his creation (38:4–38) and the animals living within it (38:39–39:30), and then describes at length the mysterious creatures Behemoth (40:15–24) and Leviathan (41:1–34). Strangely, however, God says very little directly to Job and does not say anything obvious or explicit about suffering or why he allowed Job's nightmare. This can lead to a disappointing sense of anticlimax.

It can lead to a sense of confusion, as well, because God's speeches are anything but anticlimactic for Job. After God's first speech,

Job withdraws his protest and admits he was wrong to accuse God of injustice (40:3–5), and after the second, he breaks into ecstatic worship, despising himself and caught up in a new vision of God (42:1–6). What is it that Job hears in these speeches that so profoundly reconciles him to God and God's way of running the world? As we read, let's see if we can follow Job into his happy and worshipful submission to God. Let's also consider how we might speak more wisely to ourselves and our Christian friends in suffering as a result.

God's Encouraging and Gentle Introduction (38:1–3)

It can be easy to hurry past the opening verses of chapter 38, but the way in which God initiates and structures the encounter with Job is more encouraging and gentler than you might at first think. Notice first that the Lord is introduced in a way almost identical to Job and his friends. In chapters 3–37, each new speaker is introduced with "And _____ answered and said . . ." God is here presented with almost the same phrase. This hints that he is entering the debate on its own terms, as a participant in it, and will speak in a way completely understandable to Job. This is borne out as we read God's speeches. As God asks question after question, we quickly realize that everything God asks Job is very easy to answer: the consistent answer to every question is, "Only you, Lord—only you understand or control that part of the world." God does not prolong Job's ordeal by confounding him with ineffable mysteries or stumping him with questions no mortal could answer. He rather enters into Job's world on its own terms to speak clearly and directly to his scarred servant.

At the same time, God's introduction is different because he speaks from the storm. This word can refer to purely natural storms elsewhere in the Old Testament (e.g., Ps. 107:25, 29; 148:8), and it can be easy for modern readers, unfamiliar with the symbolic terrain of the Old Testament, to assume that the storm from which God speaks is only a way of playing up divine power and majesty. This is not completely wrong. But God's appearance in the storm takes on deeper symbolic weight in the Old Testament—it is more than only a way of implying that God is really powerful. We noticed above how the raging sea and the monsters in it are common Old Testament symbols for supernatural chaos and evil (see Job 3:8; 7:12; 26:11–13). What has not yet been pointed out is that God very often appears in the storm to do battle with and defeat the unruly waters and the monsters living there (see Pss. 18:4–15; 29:3–11; 74:12–17; 89:9–10; 93:3–4; Isa. 17:12–14; 27:1; 51:9–11; Nah. 1:5–6; Hab. 3:3–15). In fact, the same word for the storm in Job 38:1 appears in Nahum 1:3, Habakkuk 3:14, and Zechariah 9:14 in exactly this connection, as God goes to war on his people's behalf against those greater powers that would swallow them. This combination is very common in the Old Testament. As often as one reads of the storming waters, one just as often reads of the Lord thundering against the waters to beat them back. This means that the Lord's awesome appearance in thunder and lightning is not a general way of speaking about divine power only. It is an Old Testament way of describing God's glorious defeat of the chaos and evil that resist his rule, all in order to save those who trust him. Although modern readers would not make this association, when God appears in the storm, it is to do battle and rescue his people. With this in mind, it is hardly an accident that God ends his second speech to Job by describing the monstrous creature Leviathan, whose dwelling is in the sea, and talks about a battle with it (41:7–8).

This means that God's appearance in 38:1 is the best of both worlds for Job: God will speak directly into Job's nightmare but does so (as it were) dressed in full battle armor, ready to go to war on Job's behalf.

God's opening question in 38:2 also would have been an encouragement to Job. "Who is this that darkens counsel by words without knowledge?" God asks. *Counsel* here means "advice" (as in Isa. 19:11) or a strategy or decision (Ps. 33:10–11; Isa. 14:26). It often refers to counsel given to the king or a strategy enacted by him as part of his rule over his realm (2 Sam. 15:31; 16:20; 1 Kings 1:12; 2 Chron. 10:13). Since God spends this speech describing creation and its animal inhabitants, the "counsel" that Job has been obscuring is probably the decisions that the divine King makes as he rules over all the created order—the policies by which he administers his world. This fits perfectly with Job's protest, for Job has been criticizing how God administers creation, claiming that God lets the wicked run free (9:22–24; 24:1). God is going to directly challenge Job's claim. Job has been darkening or obscuring God's good and fair purposes in his world. In fact, when God talks about Job obscuring counsel, God is implying that the justice and goodness of God's rule are actually manifest and easy for anyone to see, and Job should have known better than to criticize God as an uncaring tyrant. After all, if God were going to reveal some ineffable, transcendent mystery to Job, Job would not be faulted for obscuring it.[1]

The incredible gentleness and graciousness of God with his traumatized servant in this initial question is very striking. We can hear God's question as if he were asking, "Job, when you criticized

---

1 Michael Fox, "God's Answer and Job's Response," *Biblica* 94 (2013): 3.

me so viciously, did you really know what you were talking about?" This is an extraordinarily mild way to respond to someone who has portrayed God as attacking him viciously and for no reason, using Job for target practice, gnashing his teeth at him, slashing his kidneys open, grabbing him by the neck and slamming him into the ground (see 16:7–19). God probably could have been much harsher with Job: "Who is this who has railed against me so foolishly? How dare you! Get on your knees and apologize!" But the Lord instead treats his servant entirely graciously in his opening question. It is an attitude that God will maintain throughout chapters 38–41.

We should not miss how significant this would have been for Job, how clarifying and refocusing, after the fever-dream of his protest and his pain. After all, if God really were the amoral dictator Job feared, he would not have responded so gently to Job's invective. Even in his introduction, God is showing Job that he is more profoundly good and gentle than Job has given him credit for. Remember that Job feared that God might so terrify him that he would not even be able to speak (9:17–20), or that God would overwhelm him with impossible questions (9:3). None of this happens. Job's encounter with the Almighty is going to be much happier than Job ever imagined. And perhaps happiest of all is the obvious fact that when God appears, he does not accuse Job of a single sin that would explain Job's suffering—not even a hint of condemnation from the Almighty is uttered.[2] Right from the start, God is communicating that he is not angry. To appreciate how much this would have meant

---

2   If anything, the tone is the opposite—warm and perhaps even congratulatory. The particular phrasing of the opening question in v. 2 (*mî zeh*, the interrogative with the intensificatory particle) is never used elsewhere in the OT for seeking information. It usually has an awed tone (1 Sam. 17:55) and more than once expresses awe in praise of God (Ps. 24:8; Isa. 63:1; Jer. 49:19; 50:44). It is difficult to imagine God addressing Job in an awestruck tone; but is

to Job, remember that Job's deepest fear and pain in all his losses, the sharpest pang that drove all his long criticisms of God, was the thought that he had lost God's friendship and favor and did not even know why. Despite the foolish things Job has said, Job's consistent desire has been to meet with God, and God is going to fulfill that desire without crushing or berating or blasting Job. None of Job's fears are going to be realized in the encounter with God, and it will end with joys Job never imagined.

It is also worth mentioning that this is very different from how the friends thought God would treat Job. The friends were certain that when God appeared, he would decisively shut Job up (e.g., 11:5–6). When God does speak to Job, he is far gentler than either Job or the friends expected. Furthermore, God's description of his world is very different from the friends' narrow retribution theology. His speech is as much a confrontation of Job's darkest fears as it is of the friends' self-righteous certainties.

The encounter with the Lord unfolds differently from Job's expectations in another and equally significant way. Job imagined he and God could take turns speaking to each other, with Job happy to give God the first turn (13:22). God rejects this at the outset. Instead of being subjected to an interrogation by a mortal, it is the Lord who will be asking the questions and Job giving the answers (38:3). Job is not allowed any questions. This tempers the gentleness of 38:2 without muting it; God is speaking to Job "with compassion and gentleness, albeit a stern gentleness."[3] Job must "gird up his loins" (the Hebrew translated as "dress for action" in 38:3) and get ready for an encounter with the Almighty. But it

it too much to hear a warmth in God's question? As if God is proud of his servant, despite the foolish things Job has said?

3 Michael Fox, "Job 38 and God's Rhetoric," *Semeia* 18 (1981): 58.

must be this way, for if God were to submit to a cross-examination from a mortal, he would have lessened himself in so doing.[4] God will answer Job's protest, but it is not for the Almighty to justify himself under interrogation from a mortal.

The Lord establishes three things in 38:2–3: the subject of his first speech (his counsel/strategy for ruling creation, which allows for some evil); the tone (gentleness); and the means by which it will proceed (God will ask and Job will answer). God then begins his speech by turning to the world's earliest moments (38:4–7).

Where Were You When I Founded the Earth? (38:4–7)

God first questions Job about the founding of the earth. Each question has a clear and obvious answer: Job was not present when God put the world together, but God was (38:4); he cannot measure the dimensions of the earth, but God can and did (v. 5); Job does not understand that deeper stability which holds the earth in place and secures the good order and flourishing of God's world, but God does (v. 6). Of course, not all of these questions have quite the punch for a modern reader that they would have had for an ancient Semite. We now know that the earth's circumference is just under 25,000 miles. But just as many mysteries in the physical universe confront modern readers as did Job, and it would be easy for God to ask any of us similar questions: Who is the one person who understands the paradoxes of quantum mechanics? Or string theory (if that theory is correct)?

---

4   John Walton astutely points out how Job's protest has involved "pursuing options that will mean that God loses": if God either justifies himself or apologizes to Job or fails to give an explanation, God becomes less worthy of worship. "Job 1: Book of," in *Dictionary of the Old Testament: Wisdom, Poetry and Writing*, ed. Tremper Longman and Peter Enns (Downers Grove, IL: IVP Academic, 2008), 341. God does directly address Job's complaint about injustice but not within the framework of Job's expectations for an encounter with God.

The point behind these questions is not, however, to make Job feel small (something of which Job is already keenly aware [9:3]). God's intention is twofold. First, he is impressing upon his beloved servant that Job has only a very limited perspective on God's world; there is so much Job does not and cannot understand, which only God sees clearly. We have seen how, in Job's protest, he extrapolated from his tragedy in chapters 1–2 to draw sweeping conclusions about God and how he runs the world: "The earth is given into the hand of the wicked . . . if it is not he, then who is it?" (9:24). God here in chapter 38 shows that Job does not know enough about God's world to conclude that God is an unjust tyrant. When the vast amount of time between the earth's founding and Job's present existence opens up in his mind (38:4), together with the vast stretches of God's world unexplored by Job (v. 5), Job's dark certainties about God are undercut. This clears the way for Job to see God in a new way.

But God's purpose in this first passage is not only negative. God is also helping Job remember and refocus on the goodness of God's world and, by implication, the goodness of the deity who designed and rules it. We see this in the architectural metaphor in 38:5–6. Creation is commonly enough compared to a building elsewhere in the Old Testament (for example, Ps. 104:1–5; Isa. 51:13). Old Testament authors draw this comparison not to make some abstract philosophical or cosmological statement, but to play up the goodness of the stable order by which God structured created life, all so that his world can thrive and rejoice. In Psalm 104, just because God sets the world on unmovable foundations (v. 5), every living thing can flourish under God's hand (vv. 10–23). The stability of God's world in Job 38:6 thus points Job to God's protective and nurturing care of his creatures and his cosmic provision for everything he has made. A God who creates in this way cannot be the uncaring tyrant Job has railed against.

The next verse shows this even more clearly: when God created the world, beings higher than Job could not restrain themselves but broke out in joyful singing (38:7). Job earlier cursed his existence into darkness (3:3–10). Without making the connection overt, God implicitly but directly challenges Job's first speech by beginning his own first speech with joy and light, a radiant joy that erupts in the profound gloom that Job called for in chapter 3. If beings higher than Job rejoiced over God's creation, who is Job to disagree?

One more thing before we move on: some worry that God speaks in a sarcastic tone in this passage, especially in 38:5, when he says, "Surely you know!" Job has complained about his unfair treatment with such force that it can be easy to hear God speaking contemptuously to Job here, as if to humiliate him and make him sorry he ever criticized God. Detecting tone in a written text is difficult. There are, however, good reasons to see a more positive and encouraging tone in these verses and overall a much happier atmosphere permeating Job's encounter with God.[5] Note first that if verses 4–7 were all direct statements instead of questions, it would be easier to hear a more demeaning tone: "You were not there when I founded the earth, Job. You don't know its dimensions." As questions, their tone is softened somewhat. Second, the questions (in this passage and throughout chapters 38–39) are not meant to play up Job's limitations so much as point him to the one person with unlimited knowledge and mastery of the world. For example, the question in 38:5 is not, What are the dimension of the earth? but, Who is the one person who knows its dimensions? God is

---

5   In the following discussion of the tone of chap. 38, I am relying on Michael Fox's two helpful articles: "Job 38," 58–59; and "God's Answer," 3, 14.

trying to refocus Job on him, not clobber or demoralize him with impossible questions. You can see this as well in the fact that no human being would feel embarrassed for not being present at the moment of creation (38:4) or understanding the full dimensions of creation (v. 5). The point is to change Job's view of God, not score points against him in an argument.

This means that when God says, "Tell me, if you have understanding" and "Surely you know," we can imagine this in the tone of an encouraging teacher who wants the student to get it right, not someone trying to humiliate an opponent in a debate. As was already mentioned, all the questions God asks have a very easy answer: God is the only one who understands and/or controls the part of creation under discussion. In light of this, we can imagine God saying through these questions, "C'mon, Job! I know you know this!"[6]

The "Diapering" of the Sea (38:8–11)

God turns from the earth to sea in 38:8–11. The bounding and bordering of the ocean is a common theme in Old Testament creation texts (see Pss. 65:8; 89:10; 93:3–4; 104:5–9; Jer. 5:22). As with the stable founding of the earth, the limitations of the sea highlight God's goodness and protective care of his creatures. This is because the ocean is described in these poetic texts as a restless, relentless, un-organize-able force that, unless restrained, will overwhelm and annihilate all life. Job 38:8–11 fits with this broader theme perfectly, as the sea bursts forth (v. 8, probably a

---

6 In OT wisdom texts, questions are a standard means by which wisdom is passed from sage to student to help him grow, not humiliate him. Daniel Timmer, "Character Formed in the Crucible: Job's Relationship with God and Joban Character Ethics," *Journal of Theological Interpretation* 3 (2009): 10.

metaphor for God's creation of the sea) and God sets a firm limit to it (vv. 10–11). If we remember that the sea is a symbol in the Old Testament for chaos, then it makes sense that God would respond to Job's protest by turning to this common creation theme. Job has portrayed the world as a chaos where anything goes and evildoers run everything (9:22–24). According to Job, God's failure to enact justice means injustice flourishes (24:1–17). God challenges this by pointing Job to the far vaster chaotic energy that he has already immovably contained. God has already taken far greater action against a far greater chaos than Job can imagine.

There is more for Job in this passage, however. Two aspects of the poetry of 38:8–11 sharpen and beautify God's response to Job in these verses. The first is the parental imagery used: in verse 9, God literally "diapers" the sea (cf. Ezek. 16:4). Elsewhere in the Old Testament, God will thunder against the raging waters (Ps. 18:13–15) or rebuke them (Isa. 51:10) or trample them (Hab. 3:14). In Job 38:9, God cares for them like a squealing infant! Is it too much to imagine God singing the chaotic water a lullaby? Cooing to it and rocking it to sleep? Maybe. But describing the restrictions that God places on the chaotic sea as a diaper is a strikingly gentle, nurturing image. God is perfectly able to trample the raging waters when he needs to. But what profound goodness and kindness must there be in him if he treats even the raging waters as a father would a wailing infant?

The second unusual aspect in 38:8–11 that deepens our appreciation of God's goodness is the reference to the waves as "proud" at the end of verse 11. Describing them this way means that even as God gently nurtures the sea, it continues to resist him and rebel. The word elsewhere has connotations of arrogance and rebelliousness (see Job 35:12; Isa. 13:11, 19; the same image is found for the rebellious waters in Pss. 89:9; 93:3). In other words, God does not make an initial effort to care for this "child" and then give up when the storming waters fail to cooperate. His gentle care continues unstinted, regardless of how the chaos in his world fights back. This portrayal of God is worlds away from Job's dark and suspicious protest against him.

God's diapering of the sea speaks to Job's protest and reorients him in multiple ways. First, the fact that the raging waters are allowed continued existence within strict boundaries means that God's counsel or strategy for creation (38:2) is one that allows some limited agency to chaos in his world. God's world is not a perfect paradise where nothing ever goes wrong; part of God's order is to allow for some contained disorder.[7] This means God does allow some suffering in his realm. But this decision on his part does not mean that the world is the ominous and dark place Job earlier described. God both strictly limits chaos and is far kinder to it than Job ever suspected. If God treats even the rebellious waters this way, surely his goodness knows no bounds! Furthermore, although God is not directly addressing the friends, we should not miss how different this picture of God and his world is from the ones that the friends imagined: instead of a mechanistic, domino-like punishment of every misdeed, we see the continued existence of disorder in God's world—as well as God's astonishing care for it.

The Moral Edge of the Sunrise (38:12–15)

We move from the sea to the sunrise in 38:12–15. This passage describes the sunrise in some ways that are counterintuitive to modern readers but would have made more sense to ancient Semites. In

---

7   Christopher Ash, *Job: The Wisdom of the Cross*, Preaching the Word (Wheaton, IL: Crossway, 2014), 381.

these verses God describes the sunrise as shaking the wicked out of the earth, like shaking ants out of a blanket (38:13). In 38:15, the arm of the wicked is broken by the rising sun—in fact, even during sunrise they have no light.

To make sense of this, it is helpful to remember that the Old Testament associates natural and moral order more closely than modern Westerners tend to. It is easy for us to think of spiritual truths as totally divorced from impersonal scientific laws, but Old Testament authors, without making any claims that contradict modern scientific theories, think of God's created order as reflecting and aligned with spiritual realities. This is nowhere clearer than in the covenant blessings and curses of Leviticus 26 and Deuteronomy 28, where faithfulness to God and neighbor love mean large harvests and military safety for Israel—a kind of flourishing Edenic paradise. On the other hand, idolatry and unrighteousness bring military defeat and famine; creation becomes barren and unyielding. You can see the same kind of connection in texts like Psalm 112 or Proverbs 3:1–12, where righteous saints are blessed with a happy abundance as God's creatures. This is not an unscientific or barbaric way to think: haven't you noticed how mature Christians, who are practiced in trusting and obeying God, have a sort of radiance and joy to them, like flourishing plants (Ps. 92:12–15)? And this, despite and even in the midst of real suffering? That their existence as created beings is enhanced and beautified by their spiritual health?

With this in mind, it is easier to see that even if the dawn might not literally break any bones (38:15), God is reminding Job that creation has a moral edge to it. God has structured his world such that its regular patterns and orderliness work against and counteract sinful humans and their plans; the wicked cannot, as it were, get their footing (38:13) or easily accomplish their goals (v. 15; the arm is associated with strength elsewhere in the Old Testament). This is not an unscientific claim. It is not hard to think of examples of people living in rebellion against God who cannot get what they want (either because reality does not serve them or through self-sabotage). And as above, this is a direct response to Job's protest about God's supposed lack of concern for justice. Quite the contrary to Job's darkest fears, justice means so much to God that he has structured his creation so that evil has difficulty securing its place.

As above, the rhetorical questions that God uses are meant to make this conclusion inescapable for Job. Job cannot tell the sun to rise each morning, but God can and does (38:12). This is not a humiliating put-down, for no mortal would feel embarrassed for not doing this. In stating this truth as a question, God is prompting Job to conclude for himself that justice matters to God.

What Is Job Supposed to Conclude from God's First Speech?

We have surveyed only the first three passages in God's first speech, but the same patterns and emphases recur throughout all of chapters 38–39, allowing us to move more quickly through the rest of these chapters. After the sunrise, God takes Job to the outer boundaries of creation (38:16–18), to the dwelling of light and darkness (vv. 19–21), to snow and hail and the storm (vv. 22–30), to the stars (vv. 31–33), and finally the lightning (vv. 34–38). Then a variety of animals living within God's world are presented for Job: lions (38:39–41), mountain goats (39:1–4), the donkey (vv. 5–8), the wild ox (vv. 9–12), the ostrich (vv. 13–18), the war horse (vv. 19–25), and the hawk (vv. 26–30). Consistently, three unstated but clear implications are made to Job throughout.

The first has to do with Job's limitations. The world is much vaster and far stranger than Job has recognized. There is much he does not know. This means Job is not in a position to draw the sweeping generalizations about God that he has. Job cannot prove that God has been bungling his role as sovereign of the universe because there is so much of that universe he does not understand. He simply does not have enough evidence. This is especially clear as God points to the vast and unexplored dimensions of the earth (38:4–7, 16–24) as well as the ostrich, which stands as a kind of deliberate non sequitur, exposing her eggs to danger but unafraid before humans (39:13–18). If Job cannot even understand ostriches, what makes him so confident he can penetrate God's plan for guiding the entire universe and demonstrate that God is not a fair ruler? Note as well that God does not ask Job to take this on faith. Anyone can reflect on the vast dimensions of creation and the strange creatures living in it. God is gently reminding Job of a truth that he has been obscuring but which is potentially available to anyone.

Pain has a way of pulling us into ourselves, and deep pain can completely color and distort our view of the world. We can feel as if we are finally seeing the horrible truth about living in God's world, and the frightening conclusions that start to occur to us can feel unanswerable. We start to think to ourselves, "So this is what God is really like." More than a few of Job's speeches can be read this way. The first application for believers from God's first speech to Job is that no matter how unanswerable our dark suspicions about God feel, no matter how certain, we are not in a position to draw these conclusions. We just do not know enough. Strikingly, the first stage in Job's reconciliation and restoration has to do with the profound limits of his grasp of the world.

But God has far more to reveal to Job than Job's limitations. This is a good thing, for if God were only to speak to what Job does not know, he would sound suspiciously similar to the friends (see 11:5–12). While Zophar points to the limits of Job's knowledge as a way to shut him up, however, God does so so that Job will be open to the massive goodness of God's world. This is the second implication made to Job in chapters 38–39, the truth he has forgotten but should not have: that there are massive dimensions of order and goodness in God's world. It is not the sinister, creepy place Job has portrayed, and God is not the cosmic destroyer (9:5–10), but the great sustainer and provider. The angels broke into joyful singing at the sight of God's world (38:7), and God's goodness extends in unstinting care even to the rebellious chaos that he allows to exist (vv. 8–11). Job cannot make it rain, but God does so that the uninhabitable desert blossoms, and man and beast can thrive there (38:25–27).

God's goodness is also clear from those animals that God feeds but which would have been dangerous for Job even to approach (such as the lion of 39:39–40) or would have been counted as unclean in the Old Testament (such as the raven in 39:41 or the hawk in 39:26–30). Predators like lions and scavengers, like ravens or hawks, would easily have come in contact with blood, so Israelites would have done everything possible to avoid them (see Lev. 11:13–19; 17:10–12). Some animals are integrated neatly into Israel's communal life and regular worship, such as livestock, which are included in the Sabbath command (Ex. 20:10). But many of the animals in the Lord's first speech to Job are far outside the ordered sphere of covenant life and live in the strange and dangerous waste places of desert and mountain. Despite this, God's care extends no less to them than those animals more familiar to Job. This means God is more profoundly good than Job has claimed. God's goodness simply cannot be contained to the familiar dimensions of farms and villages where most Israelites lived. In fact, it means that even the more sinister aspects of God's world, such as lions that could easily kill Job (38:39–40) or the war horse that could trample him (39:19–25), become themselves signposts of God's goodness, while still being dangerous and unnerving. It is not just the hearth and home where Job is safe. Even those wilder and threatening parts of God's world stand under God's nurturing care. There is not a single square inch of God's world, not a single animal living in it (whether easily domesticated, dangerous, or just plain weird) that does not witness to God's unstinting care and goodness.

This must mean that God cannot be the violent bully against whom Job earlier protested (16:9–17). But God does not explicitly make this connection; he leaves the implication unstated. A moment's reflection shows why this must be so. If God were specifically to tell Job about his goodness to Job and care of him, it would sound too much like a parent trying to pacify a child having a temper tantrum.[8] God implies his profound goodness to Job on the basis of his care of everything in creation (a truth potentially available to any human being) and expects Job to draw the right conclusion.

A third implication of God's first speech is that there is some chaos that God allows to exist in his world. We do not yet live in the new creation, where the sea is no more (Rev. 21:1), and crying and pain and death are distant memories (v. 4). Part of God's present plan for his world is to allow some continued existence and some limited agency to chaos and evil. The sea is barred, but still rages (Job 38:9–11); storms might still sink a ship (vv. 34–35); lions remain dangerous (vv. 39–40). God does not immediately stop every threatening aspect of his world but allows pockets of chaos to exist within a much larger order.

8 Fox, "God's Answer," 15.

This introduces an element of realism to chapters 38–39 that prevents any impression that the world is being presented in a romantic or idealistic way. God does not view the world through rose-tinted glasses and does not ask Job to. In pointing to the sea and dangerous predators, God is implying that his royal policy for creation does allow for some suffering. This does not at all mean that he is the uncaring tyrant of Job's protests, or his world a moral free-for-all. But God's world does have a wildness that is sometimes frightening and sometimes dangerous. God does not explicitly draw conclusions from this for Job, but I think it speaks to Job's protest in multiple ways. First, Job could infer that God understands the suffering Job has borne; because God is aware and in control of the sea, we can hear God whispering to Job, "I know what you've been through, my son, and I know the chaos that destroyed your life." (Remember that Job asked in 7:12 why God was treating him like the sea or the monster that lives there.) Job also could infer that not all suffering is punishment and that his own tragedy is not unassailable evidence of God's hatred of and hostility toward him. In other words, as God describes the chaotic elements in his world without a hint of condemnation toward Job, God severs Job's linking of his tragedy with inexplicable divine anger toward him. In the complex and mysterious interworking of God's world, as massive and joyful goodness surrounds some menacing elements, Job can conclude that God does allow for contained (if intense) suffering without necessarily approving of it or directly inflicting it on people as punishment. This means that Job need not add to his pain by interpreting it as a guilty verdict from his divine friend.

We could summarize God's challenge to Job's protest in the following way. Job's protest against God's unjust rule (made on the basis of what appeared to be unjustified punishment) is unwarranted for three reasons: it was made without sufficient evidence, in the face of the massive goodness in God's rule, and without accounting for the way God both contains and cares for even the chaos he allows to continue to exist. Job may not yet know why he suffered; but he does know that God is not angry with him and that his ordeal was not a case of God punishing a good man as a terrible sinner. He also knows that God's rule is far more joyful than Job ever imagined.

It is important to remember that this is not a timeless defense of God's justice in the face of evil. We shouldn't necessarily enlist Job 38–39 in our apologetic arguments to non-Christians. God's first speech is made specifically in response to Job's protest. It is meant to sever and disrupt Job's dark certainties about God and open Job's mind and heart to a joy and goodness he had never considered, even in the midst of a sometimes dangerous world. Furthermore, God accomplishes this not through an abstract or logical argument, but through vivid poetry: the sunrise reveals the earth's topography like clay shaped under a seal impression (38:14); Job is given a glimpse, beyond the world's horizon, beyond the reach of mortal sight, of the very gates of death (v. 17); the warhorse's neck is clothed with (literally) "thunder," as he laughs where soldiers would fear and paws the ground, snorting, muscles tense (39:19–22). This means modern readers, whether themselves suffering or trying to be faithful friends to Christians who are, should take their time with the images and let their imaginations go to work. Try to ask yourself the sorts of questions God might put to you, if you were given an encounter like Job's. Did you know about the supermassive black hole in the galaxy cluster Abell 85, apparently forty billion times the mass of the sun—the same mass as almost two-thirds of all the stars in that galaxy? Who is the one person who could sustain a void so unimaginably huge? Who is the one person who sees every iota of the inner stretches of that black hole clearly—a place no human could ever penetrate without being destroyed, from which not even light can escape? Or let's move from the huge to the microscopic. Just as God names all the billions of stars in his universe (Isa. 40:26), who is the one person who knows by name every molecule in your body—every atom—every subatomic particle? Who is the one person who sustains each as part of his intimate care for you and does so even as you criticize him? Who sustains the very synapses in your brain that allow you to think and articulate your complaint about how badly he has treated you?

Or consider the Inuit. Did you know that it is estimated that people first moved above the arctic circle around five thousand years ago? Who is the one person who has been sustaining them all this time? Who put the world together so that people could live in a climate so inhospitable that one would think nothing at all could survive there? Does that sound like the work of an unfeeling, untrustworthy bully to you?

Or we could consider some animals. Did you know that the mantis shrimp has one of the most complex sets of eyes in the animal kingdom, with twelve photoreceptors in comparison to the three that human eyes have, allowing them to see ultraviolet light? Or that they have bony appendages that they can use, moving at about 32 feet (10 meters) per second, to punch their prey, with the power of a .22-caliber bullet? Who is the one person who could invent an animal like that? Or what about the elephants that came to the house of Lawrence Anthony, a conservationist who had worked to protect them, one year to the day after he died? How did the elephants know to do that? And who is the one person who could create a creature like that?

Take your darkest suspicions that God is not really a good person and expose them to questions of this kind. Is it plausible to think he is incompetent at best or (at worst) malicious? Job claims the beasts of the field and the birds of the air teach God's injustice (12:7–9). Very well: consider the lion and raven, the ostrich and hawk from Job 39, or the mantis shrimp and the elephant. Job's speeches have the momentum of one clearing away all superficial comforts and shallow half-truths. If you find yourself agreeing with his protests, allow the momentum of his questions to propel you (guided by God's first speech) into a new vision of God. Keep sweeping away all half-truths about God as you listen to the questions of Job 38–39 until you can see him in a totally new light. Or if you are speaking to a suffering friend, perhaps you can find the right time and the right way to ask, "I understand why you would be saying these things about God. But come, do they really bear up under scrutiny? Do you know enough to say that? Could the kind of person you're describing invent a sunset? Or music? Or a lion?"

This is what C. S. Lewis did in the agony of his wife's death and the spiritual darkness that settled on him as a result. Although he never quotes the book of Job in *A Grief Observed*, he sounds uncannily like Job on more than one occasion, such as when he admits:

Not that I am (I think) in much danger of ceasing to believe in God. The real danger is of coming to believe such dreadful things about Him. The conclusion I dread is not, "So there's no God after all," but, "So this is what God's really like. Deceive yourself no longer."[9]

---

9   C. S. Lewis, *A Grief Observed* (repr., New York: Bantam, 1976), 5.

Lewis's torture grows so intense that later in the book he calls God a vivisectionist and "the Cosmic Sadist, the spiteful imbecile"— perhaps the grimmest and most disturbing sentence that the most celebrated Christian writer of the twentieth century ever wrote.[10] But no sooner are the words put to paper than he questions them: "Is it rational to believe in a bad God?"[11] And when Lewis puts the question that way, he finds it impossible to do so. He thinks of a terrible man he once knew who used to boast to Lewis about how he would torture animals. Lewis concludes:

> Now a being [like that man], however magnified, couldn't invent or create or govern anything. He would set traps and try to bait them. But he'd never have thought of baits like love, or laughter, or daffodils, or a frosty sunset. *He* make a universe? He couldn't make a joke, or a bow, or an apology, or a friend.[12]

Our darkest fears of God can feel terribly certain in the midst of suffering. In God's gentle way, he dismantles them by pointing to evidence anyone can see, all without blaming us. God is incomprehensibly greater and kinder, and his world more wild, more dangerous, and more beautiful, than we have yet considered.

Job's Response and Ours (40:3–5)

Earlier Job predicted that if God would just stop being so distant and mysterious, he would argue his ways right to God's face (13:15; 23:3–6). Job was wrong: everything in Job's first response shows his submission before God, his rejection of his former protest, and

10 Lewis, *A Grief Observed*, 33, 35.
11 Lewis, *A Grief Observed*, 35.
12 Lewis, *A Grief Observed*, 35–36.

his agreement with the justice of God's rule over all things. Hand over mouth, he has absolutely nothing more to add to his protest. God is right; Job is wrong.

This is a good response, and even a shocking one, after Job's persistence (one might even say defiance) in seeking an encounter with the God whom he thinks wronged him so terribly. But in comparison with Job's second response, it feels a little cold. In 42:1–6, Job engages in beautiful and heartbroken worship; here, he only admits he's insignificant before God and was wrong to protest. Is there still some reticence in Job? He admits his protest against God's irrational hostility and needless anger toward him was wrong. So far, so good. But perhaps Job is not quite ready to trust God fully again. There still seems some distance that needs bridging.

There may be some lingering coldness in the reader, as well. It is fine to talk about the sunrise and ostriches when one is tempted toward unfounded conclusions about God—but Job has dead children. If this were all God had to say, we might know that he is still a good person; but it might also be hard to feel really safe around him.

Fortunately, God has a more profound breakthrough waiting for Job and for the patient reader as well. But Job must be shown Behemoth and Leviathan up close before he can enter into that deep worship of God that is the only true healing of his wounds.

What Have We Learned?

1. God's response in Job 38–39 is not a timeless defense of his policies but a specific response to Job's protest and the sorts of things people will say in Job-like ordeals. These chapters are not a general, philosophical answer to the problem of evil

but a gentle challenge to sufferers who wonder if God is at best incompetent and at worst malicious.

2. God is far gentler with Job (and with later sufferers) than we might imagine. Without ignoring the unwise things Job has said, God is incredibly gracious with his scarred servant—itself a proof that Job's darkest suspicions of God are untrue.

3. Our first step in wisdom is humility: there is so much we do not know. The limitations of our grasp of God's world urges humility in hasty conclusions about incompetence or malice on the part of the deity who guides every part, even suffering and evil.

4. Pain can so contract and color our vision of the world that all we see is tragedy. God redirects us in chapters 38–39 so that we can appreciate the awesome goodness and beauty in his world and the divine King who rules it. No matter how we might feel that tragedy and loss are the real truth of existence, God shows that joy and goodness are the dominant theme in his world.

5. God's plan for his world is not some perfect paradise where nothing goes wrong; he does allow some predators in the animal world, and does allow some suffering for his children. But far from proving God's injustice, these dangerous elements that he sustains in creation are themselves surrounded by his goodness. If God cares not just for puppies and horses but for animals dangerous to humans or even incomprehensible, surely his care will surround you when danger interrupts your life, in ways you cannot understand?

6

Behemoth, Leviathan, and God's Defeat of Evil

(Job 40:6–41:34)

GOD'S FIRST SPEECH SHOWED an almost bewildering variety in his tour of the cosmos and the animal world. His second speech is simpler: after the preparation of the divine warrior (40:8–14), he describes the monsters Behemoth (vv. 15–24) and Leviathan (41:1–34). Just as in his first speech, God does not draw any explicit conclusions from these descriptions. This means that we will have to continue to listen very closely for what Job heard that reduced him to worship (42:1–6). Another similarity to the first speech is that God's initial questions in 40:7–8 are crucial for understanding the speech as a whole. Let's consider them first.

Will You Break My Justice? (40:7–8)

God introduces his second speech in 40:7 by repeating the command that Job gird up his loins (see 38:3). Just as in the first speech,

God will be the one asking the questions and Job the one answering. Instead of telling Job that Job has been darkening counsel, however, God now asks Job whether Job is right to "break God's justice" (40:8).[1] To break means to frustrate, invalidate, or deny something (see Job 5:12; 15:4; Ps. 89:34). This is exactly what Job has done in the course of the debate—denied that God is just, fair, and good. The second question in 40:8 ("Will you condemn me that you may be in the right?") also directly responds to Job's protest. Job's limited perspective on the tragedy of chapters 1–2 has meant that he wrongly but understandably interpreted his losses as punishment from God. This leaves him with only two options in trying to comprehend and resolve his suffering: either God was right and Job is a sinner deserving to lose all the blessings of obedience, or Job was innocent all along and God mishandled Job's case (at best) or maliciously tortured an innocent man (at worst). Since Job knows he truly is innocent, he has pursued the second option in his speeches. This means that when God asks, "Will you condemn me that you may be in the right?" God is widening Job's perspective so that suffering can occur without the sufferer being blamed as deserving of pain or God being smeared as an uncaring tyrant. God is, in other words, going to help Job see that suffering can occur, God can be just, and Job can be innocent all at the same time.[2] Put differently, Job has (understandably but mistakenly) interpreted his suffering such that either he is God's enemy (7:12) or God is his (16:9–17). God will use his second

---

1 The ESV translates this less literally as "Will you even put me in the wrong?" This is a good translation, but rendering it more literally is preferable because it brings the issue of God's justice to the forefront—exactly the issue in Job's protest.

2 J. C. L. Gibson, "On Evil in the Book of Job," in *Ascribe to the Lord: Biblical and Other Essays in Memory of Peter C. Craigie,* Journal for the Study of the Old Testament Supplemental Series 67 (Sheffield: JSOT Press, 1988), 401.

speech to unmask the real enemy and show Job how he will defeat it.[3] This will open a much happier horizon in which, despite his terrible losses, Job is still innocent and God still his friend. As we read God's initial questions in 40:7–8, we learn that he has listened closely to his scarred servant protest and is giving a direct answer. God presses more deeply into Job's complaint in his second speech and demonstrates his perfect justice and goodness, despite the presence of at times horrific evil in his world.

The Preparation of the Divine Warrior (40:9–14)

We mentioned in the last chapter how God's appearance in the storm (38:1) would have been deeply significant for an ancient Semite like Job because it would have communicated God's warfare on Job's behalf. A similar note is sounded in 40:9–14. When God asks Job about his arm and thunderous voice (40:9) and adorning himself with glorious splendor (v. 10), this echoes many other Old Testament passages that show the Lord radiating a numinous, awesome glory as he goes to battle to save his people from powers (human or supernatural) that would defeat and enslave them (see Ex. 6:6; 15:16; Pss. 29:2; 89:11; 93:1; 96:6; 104:1–2; Isa. 30:30; 51:9–11). Just as in the storm at the beginning of the first speech, God's initial questions in 40:9–10 have to do not with divine power in a general sense but with the glorious activation of that power on behalf of the helpless as God saves those who trust him and makes his world right again. This is exactly how the rest of 40:9–14 plays out: after the questions of verses 9–10, God describes his just judgment of sinners (v. 12) on a level and to an extent that Job could never accomplish—a sentence of eternal death (v. 13). As

---

3 Robert Fyall, *Now My Eyes Have Seen You: Images of Creation and Evil in the Book of Job*, New Studies in Biblical Theology 12 (Downers Grove, IL: InterVarsity Press, 2002), 141.

in chapters 38–39, God asks these questions not to humiliate Job, for no mortal would ever claim to be able to enact justice on this scale. He is prompting Job to conclude for himself that God both can and does execute justice, and gloriously so. It is the wicked (40:12) who fall under God's judgment, not Job. Will Job continue to insist that God is negligent at best and malicious at worst when God is, even now, looking on everyone who is proud and bringing them low? Will Job break God's justice (40:8)?

"The wicked" in 40:12 refers to human evildoers (see Job 3:17; 8:22; 11:20; 38:13; Ps. 1:1; Eccles. 8:10; and elsewhere). God does not limit the execution of his justice to the human realm, however. The rest of his speech describes Behemoth and Leviathan, two creatures that (as we will see) represent supernatural chaos and evil. This means that the different parts of God's second speech cohere in such a way that Job can see God adorning himself with splendor and majesty (40:10) and readying his weapons of warfare (v. 9), both to execute justice and usher in blessing and *shalom* in the human realm (vv. 11–13), and also on a more-than-human scale, gloriously defeating those sinister powers of chaos and evil that would otherwise destroy God's world (represented by Behemoth and Leviathan in 40:15–24 and 41:1–34). This is the high point of God's word to Job—but, as elsewhere, God does not make this conclusion explicit. It's as if he wants Job to see Leviathan up close and draw for himself the right conclusions about God and his world.

I'd like us to do the same. Although I have already made clear how I interpret these chapters, I want to follow the lead of the text and simply listen to these long descriptions. As much as possible, I want to enter into the position of someone hearing them for the first time. It appears that God wants us to attend very closely to these two monsters. It is difficult to understand why else he would describe them at such length, for elsewhere in the Old Testament, physical descriptions are extremely brief—usually a phrase or two (see, for example, Gen. 29:17 or 1 Sam. 16:12). In contrast, Behemoth gets nine verses and Leviathan a whopping thirty-four!

We've already sat with Job in the dust and listened to his grief. Now let's listen with him as he gets a close-up tour of two terrifying monsters—and sees God in a whole new way as a result.

Behemoth and Leviathan Up Close (40:15–24; 41:1–34)

When the Lord says to Job, "Behold, Behemoth," in 40:15 and describes a big animal in a river, we of course do not need to imagine a literal river flowing next to the ash heap where Job was scraping his sores (2:8). But as God paints for Job a series of verbal images, each as vivid as the last, we can engage with them in an appropriately imaginative way by picturing the Lord directing Job's attention (in his mind's eye) to a wide river and a hulking shape that lies there, half-submerged, covered in shadow by overhanging trees. As we look, we see a massive, brutal beast of an animal, an unmovable strength, thick muscles interwoven over bones like bars of iron (40:17–18). It just lies there, unmoving, unblinking, staring at us from the dappled shadow of lotus plants (40:21–22). Suddenly there is a cry nearby from another animal. Birds take to flight in a rustle of feather and fish dart away, but Behemoth is unperturbed, unmoving, silent, lurking (40:23). One look at the creature, and you know it wouldn't even flinch before the normal ways human capture and control other animals (40:24). All the other animals know it too: poetically, they bring tribute before their king (40:20).

This is not, however, just an ancient version of a nature documentary. In 40:19, the Lord speaks of bringing a sword against this creature. God does not elaborate on this, but it is a crucial verse to remember so that we can make sense out of why God directs our attention to Behemoth. We will pick this up again below.

In chapter 41, we leave the lurking brawn of Behemoth and turn our gaze toward the sea, where the normally calm water breaks into boiling and bubbling as a massive, thrashing monstrosity rises to the surface. Job knows, in a distant way, about Leviathan (see 3:8), but God is going to give Job an up-close tour of the creature in the longest physical description in all the Bible. No sooner is Leviathan introduced in 41:1 than Job already knows he is completely powerless before this writhing energy; none of the normal ways humans capture crocodiles stand a chance against Leviathan (vv. 1–2). It is beyond ridiculous to imagine Leviathan begging Job for mercy or trying to cut a deal with him to let him go (41:3–4), and just as ridiculous to imagine Job keeping the creature as a pet or selling him (vv. 5–6). A single encounter would be more than enough to convince Job that he could never go to battle with Leviathan—even to touch the creature would be the experience of a lifetime (41:7–8). A glimpse of the tumult and turmoil of Leviathan is enough to turn back any potential attacker—even keeping your feet is difficult when this monster is nearby (41:9).

Job may have had difficulty keeping his feet (so to speak) as God brings Leviathan near, but the Almighty has only begun to show Job the terrible proportions of this creature. Is it too much to imagine Job's eyes growing wide and a shiver traveling down his spine as he sees terror around its teeth (41:14), scales knit like armor (vv. 15–17), numinous, fiery lightning flashing from its mouth (vv. 18–21), all beneath mysterious, glowing eyes (v. 18)? Terror dances around Leviathan's unbending neck (41:22); weapons are about as useful as straw (vv. 26–28). As the creature swims away, its sharp, scaly underside makes the deep boil like a pot (41:32–33).

Why does the Lord continue at such length about how no one could possibly attack or subdue Leviathan, and what does this have to do with the explicit subject of the Lord's second speech—his justice (40:8)? We get a clue in 41:10: "No one is so fierce that he dares to stir [Leviathan] up. Who then is he who can stand before me?" In this verse, God includes himself in an unequal comparison with Leviathan: if humans are utterly helpless before the monster, then we are infinitely helpless before God.

This is only one verse in a long chapter, but it is crucial for rightly discerning why God goes on at such length about this creature. We see in verse 10 that even though God says very little directly about himself in chapter 41, the momentum and torque of the whole chapter is meant to make Job see God differently: if Leviathan is unapproachably fierce, Leviathan's Creator is infinitely more so. Every verse about Leviathan is meant to help Job see God as even more gloriously and unsurpassably indomitable than the monster. So far, so good—but why would God impress this on Job at such length and with such intensity? Isn't Job already painfully aware of how outmatched he is by God (9:2–20)? Some take the point to be that because God is even fiercer than Leviathan, Job should stop criticizing God.[4] But Job has already admitted he was wrong to protest and withdrawn his protest (40:3–5), so if this is all the Lord is saying, his second speech is redundant. Furthermore, why would a demonstration of God's unapproachable fierceness alone reduce Job to worship?

The comparison between God and Leviathan in 41:10 is only one verse, but it makes us read the entire chapter differently because it

---

4 John Walton argues this way (*Job*, NIV Application Commentary [Grand Rapids, MI: Eerdmans, 2012], 413). One problem with this interpretation is that if God is only implying to Job that Job needs to stop protesting, this says nothing about justice (40:8).

shows us that every line of poetry about Leviathan is meant to help us see Leviathan's maker differently. But God does not explicitly tell Job what new insight Job is supposed to receive, an insight so profound that it obliterates all of Job's protests and reduces him to worship. What is it that Job heard in this speech that so radically changed his view of God?

One way to approach this question is to consider a common interpretation of Behemoth and Leviathan, as well as some significant problems with it. This will, in turn, lead us into a better understanding of the two monsters described at such length in Job 40–41 and help us see their Creator in the way he intends us to see him.

Behemoth and Leviathan as Ordinary Animals or Symbols of Supernatural Chaos and Evil

You are probably already aware that Behemoth and Leviathan are most commonly taken as descriptions of a hippopotamus and a crocodile; for most modern Westerners, this is our default interpretation of the ending of Job. When read this way, the point to Job is usually taken to be that the hippo and crocodile display the wisdom and power of God, and as a result, Job should not criticize God's supposed injustice but instead submit to and trust him.

This way of reading the ending of Job has some very wise interpreters of the book on its side.[5] There are so many problems with it, however, that it is almost certainly wrong. Most importantly, this interpretation cannot explain why Job reacts so differently to

5 See, e.g., David Atkinson, *The Message of Job* (Downers Grove, IL: InterVarsity Press, 1991), 151; Robert Alden, *Job*, New American Commentary 11 (Nashville: Broadman & Holman, 1993), 400; Tremper Longman, *Job*, Baker Commentary on the Old Testament Wisdom and Psalms (Grand Rapids, MI: Baker Academic, 2016), 441–45.

God's second speech in comparison to his first, for why would a hippo and a crocodile move Job from merely admitting he was wrong (40:3–5) to abject worship (42:1–6)? The first speech already described animals that were impressive enough to display the wisdom and power of God. If Behemoth and Leviathan are just two more ordinary animals, why does Job react so differently to them? Furthermore, what do a hippo and a crocodile have to do with God's justice (40:8)?

The names of the creatures present another problem for a purely naturalistic interpretation. "Behemoth" is actually an Anglicization of the feminine plural form of the Hebrew word *bĕhēmāh*, which refers to animals in general or livestock in particular. *Behemoth* is thus literally "beasts." Hebrew uses plural nouns in places where English does not. One such use is called a "plural of majesty," in which a single subject is referred to with a plural to portray it as majestic or impressive. This is usually how the plural is taken here: we should read not "beasts" but "*the* beast" or "Superbeast."[6] This suggests that God is not describing any one species in particular by referring to Behemoth in 40:15 and fits better with understanding Behemoth as a symbol, not an ordinary hippo.

The name Leviathan points in the same direction, because Leviathan elsewhere refers to a supernatural chaos monster, not an ordinary animal. Job himself refers to Leviathan in this way in 3:8; you can see the same in Isaiah 27:1 and Psalm 74:14.[7] This means that if God means to present Behemoth and Leviathan as ordinary animals, he is doing so in a very confusing way!

---

6   See Christopher Ash, *Job: The Wisdom of the Cross*, Preaching the Word (Wheaton, IL: Crossway, 2014), 410.

7   Ps. 104:26 seems to be an exception to this, but may not be; see more discussion in Eric Ortlund, "The Identity of Leviathan and the Meaning of the Book of Job," *Trinity Journal* 34 (2013): 19–23.

Consider as well how the rhetorical questions in 40:24 and 41:1–7 collapse if ordinary animals are in view. This is the case because ancient Egyptians can and did capture hippos and crocodiles. As a result, if God is asking these questions only about two ordinary animals, Job could reply that even if he had not personally thrown a harpoon at a crocodile (41:7), human beings often do. These creatures must be more than natural for God's rhetorical questions to have any force.

Furthermore, why would God need to adorn himself with glory and thunder with his voice (40:9–10) and bring his sword near (v. 19) to an ordinary hippo? Why would he speak of a battle with Leviathan (40:7–8) and emphasize so repeatedly that it is a battle no human can even think of winning (vv. 8–9, 25–29)? It is far more satisfying to read Job 40–41 in harmony with the common Old Testament theme of the Lord's theophanic defeat of chaos. Doing so explains why Job worships so profoundly in response. Job thought God was attacking him for no reason. Now he learns that the person he has been criticizing is actually going to battle against a monster Job can barely imagine!

One reason why it is natural to assume that Behemoth and Leviathan are ordinary animals is the way God emphasizes that he is their Creator. When God says, "Behold, Behemoth, which I made as I made you; he eats grass like an ox" (40:15), it's easy to picture a big, ox-like creature standing next to Job[8]—an ordinary animal that would have been made on the fifth day of creation, just as Job was on the sixth (40:15; in 41:33, Leviathan is named as a creature

---

8   That Behemoth eats grass like an ox may, however, very well have had altogether different connotations for ancient Israelites, for some of the monsters in ancient Middle Eastern texts are described as consuming vegetation. See Robert Fyall, *Now My Eyes Have Seen You*, 133–36.

as well).[9] It is important that we notice how both Behemoth and Leviathan are creations of God, because the text emphasizes it. But instead of concluding that this means Behemoth and Leviathan are ordinary animals, keeping in mind Israel's polytheistic context can helpfully explain why this emphasis is made. In ancient Middle Eastern paganism, no one god was ultimate or transcendent, but rather a variety of gods, some good and some chaotic, vied for supremacy. This meant that the ultimate triumph of light over darkness was by no means assured, for darkness and chaos were a part of the divine nature. In fact, Leviathan himself was known outside of Israel as a chaos monster that the Canaanite storm god Baal had defeated.[10]

This means that as God describes Behemoth and Leviathan in ways that constantly suggest they are more than natural creatures, it is very important that God guard against any misunderstanding on the part of ancient Israelites that these chaotic powers were competitor gods—especially when the historical books show how easily Israel fell into pagan ways of thinking. This helps us understand that God is accomplishing two goals in the Behemoth and Leviathan speech. First, he is revealing to Job the supernatural chaos and evil that God allows in his world, which is the source of suffering and pain. At the same time, God is clarifying that an infinite divide exists between God the Creator and everything else in reality, whether Job himself, or the ordinary animals from chapter 39, or those more sinister powers that rebel against God in chapters 40–41. Whether it is an ant, a human being, or a fallen

---

9 The word in this verse correctly translated as "creature" is actually a passive participle of the verb "to make" ('āsah), that is, "a thing made."

10 Those interested can read more about this in my "The Identity of Leviathan and the Meaning of the Book of Job," 18–19.

angel, each belongs in the "creature" category in relation to God. (Please understand that when I call chaos "supernatural" in this book, I mean that these chaotic powers are higher than Job, and certainly not on the same level as God.) In other words, Behemoth and Leviathan, although unmasterable by any human being, in no way threaten the transcendent uniqueness of God and his entirely good and kind purposes for his world. As vast a divide separates Job from the infinite Creator as separates Leviathan from God.[11]

To summarize the progress we have made so far: God's second speech has explicitly to do with his justice (40:8). Behemoth and Leviathan are best understood not as ordinary animals but as

---

11 When I teach the book of Job, someone usually asks at this point whether, because God created Behemoth and Leviathan and they symbolize evil, God created evil. It is natural to ask this sort of question but much more difficult to answer because it raises larger theological and even philosophical questions. Nevertheless, I am very uncomfortable with saying that God created evil. It seems to me that part of what Gen. 1 reveals is that evil was in no way a part of God's original creation, and creation could have blossomed perfectly without any element of evil being present at all. This would have been revelatory in the ancient world, which thought of evil and chaos and death as an ineradicable part of the fabric of things. Gen. 1 is one way that God helps us toward a much more joyful view of his world, in which we can see that all mourning and crying and pain (Rev. 21:4) are only temporary intruders that will one day be banished. Besides, I am not even sure evil is the kind of thing that can be created. Does darkness need to be brought into existence? Surely it is only an absence of light? Similarly, I find it helpful to think of sin not as a positive thing that needs to be created, but only a perverting and diminution of the good God does create.

All this may seem to cut against the plain statement in Job 40:15 that God created Behemoth along with Job. Note, however, that there are indications that Behemoth and Leviathan are not animal species at all; I know of no species fitting Behemoth's description that has a tail like a cedar (v. 17), and certainly no species that, like Leviathan, breathes fire (41:18–21) and swims deep into the ocean (vv. 31–32). Behemoth and Leviathan seem to be purely symbolic (unlike the serpent of Gen. 3, which was a real species inhabited by the devil). In naming Behemoth and Leviathan creatures of God, the text is not implying that evil comes from God, but rather clarifying that whatever evil has come to exist in the world is unambiguously on one side of the infinite distance between Creator and creation. Although rebellion against God can occur in the human or angelic realms (cf. Rev. 12:9), and although Behemoth and Leviathan are appropriate symbols for the evil at loose in creation, these powers always and forever exist only under God's transcendent rule.

symbols of chaotic powers that rebel against God. Their long description is, however, not so much meant to make Job focus on Behemoth and Leviathan themselves as much as to help Job see God differently (41:10). The exact way in which Job is supposed to see God differently is not made explicitly clear in these chapters, however, even though Job does confess a profound new insight into God in the next chapter (42:1–6). God describes them for a long time and then stops talking. So what new conclusions does Job draw about God and his world after his guided tour of Behemoth and Leviathan?

What Does Job Learn from the Lord's Second Speech?

I think the Lord's second speech would have spoken volumes to Job. To begin with, God reveals to Job a massive, writhing evil at loose in God's world—a more than human chaos that Job knows distantly (3:8) but God sees up close. In fact, the uniquely long description of Leviathan is showing Job that God is more acutely aware of everything wrong with his world than Job ever could be. Earlier, Job had wondered why times for judgment were never held by the Almighty (24:1), but as God shows Job Leviathan's teeth and scaly hide and fiery breath up close, any thought that God is unaware of or unconcerned about what is wrong with his world vanishes from Job's mind forever. Job thought he had seen the ugliest side of life in his suffering. Now he realizes he has not seen the half of it—but God does.

God's revelation of Leviathan to Job would also have been helpful in clarifying to Job that God is not his enemy, nor treating Job as an enemy. We noticed above how Job's limited perspective means he sometimes portrays God as an agent of chaos or wonders why God is treating himself as one. In describing Leviathan at such length, God is helpfully complicating Job's theology such that terrible suffering and pain can occur without God being directly responsible. God unmasks Job's real enemy, and his own. Imagine what relief would have flooded Job's heart as he realized that all his wild fears about God being irrationally angry with him, all his heartache over his apparently lost friendship with God, were all entirely mistaken—his suffering did not mean God was angry!

God is also helpfully complicating the theology of the friends. Because God's plan for his creation is to allow for some elements of chaos within a much larger order, sometimes suffering will occur without there being any sin that would explain it. Leviathan's presence in God's world means that no tight connection can be made between suffering and sin.

Furthermore, it seems to me that the long description of Leviathan is God's way of implying to Job that he understands how profoundly Job has suffered. In fact, God may be saying to Job that God is the only one who sees the true dimensions of Job's suffering. Job thought he was clobbered by God for no reason. God shows him that Job has been caught up in a massive war in heaven. Not only is God intimately aware of the evil at loose in his world; he is intimately aware of everything that went wrong with Job's life—more so than Job ever could be. God is definitely not the distant, uncaring tyrant Job had worried about.

Most importantly, God reveals to Job in the Behemoth and Leviathan speeches that he will one day defeat the supernatural evil that he presently tolerates. Behemoth and Leviathan are meant to be terrifying: the merest sight of the monster would make us tremble (41:9). But there is coming a day when God will bring his sword near (40:19) and engage in a battle that no human could (41:7–8). Remember that all the rhetorical questions in chapters

38–39 point not to things God might hypothetically do but actually does every day, such as commanding the sunrise (38:12), sending rain (vv. 25–28), or feeding lions (vv. 39–40). The rhetorical questions surrounding Leviathan have the same force: Job cannot fill his hide with harpoons or lay hands on him in battle, but God can and will (41:7–8).

In other words, the one person who most clearly sees what is wrong with his world is the one person who promises he will not let it stay this way forever. There is coming a day when God will gloriously scour every last trace of evil from his world and make all things new. Job cannot so much as lay a finger on Leviathan—but Leviathan cannot so much as lay a finger on God (41:10). The coming battle will be entirely one-sided. This is God's justice (40:8).

This is, of course, a very different answer from the sorts of answers Christians typically give in response to inexplicable evil and suffering—answers that are not wrong in themselves, and certainly not without scriptural support. God says nothing about all things working together for good, true as that is (Rom. 8:28). He says nothing about guiding evil for his own good purposes, true as that is (Gen. 50:20). He says nothing about the glories of the eschaton overwhelming all the sufferings of this present age, true as that is (2 Cor. 4:17). He only tells Job that he is entirely aware of the problem—more so than Job ever could be—and will one day defeat and destroy the evil he presently tolerates. This speaks directly to Job's protest, of course. But there is also a great deal that God does not explain. He does not justify to Job his decision to allow some evil on the basis of greater good that could not be brought about any other way. I do believe, of course, that God does bring greater good out of the evil that he presently tolerates. But that truth forms no part of his answer to Job. This means that just as the book of

Job reveals to us a unique sort of ordeal that God sometimes allows, so God's climactic answer to suffering is unique in all of Scripture. God does not justify or explain himself to Job. God promises Job victory, and that is all. As we will see, this is enough for Job, and more than enough.

The Joy of the Divine Warrior

There is one more aspect of the Leviathan speech that has not been mentioned so far, but which we should not miss. In 41:12, God says, "I will not keep silence concerning his limbs, or his mighty strength, or his goodly frame." This verse transitions from the rhetorical questions of 41:1–11 to the physical description of verses 13–34 and colors how we read the rest of the chapter. It is an oddly positive thing to say about the monster God will one day defeat. Why would God describe Leviathan as having a "goodly frame"? The word translated "goodly" is used elsewhere to describe favor and grace with God (Ps. 84:12; Prov. 3:4; Zech. 12:10), or it can refer to some pleasing attribute in more general ways (Prov. 5:19; Eccles. 10:12). It almost sounds like God is praising his opponent! Why does God do this?

To speak to Leviathan's "goodly frame" cannot be a way of saying that Leviathan itself is good, because everything that follows 41:12 in verses 13–34 has to do with how unapproachably dangerous and violent and frightening Leviathan is. So when God speaks of Leviathan's "mighty strength" and "goodly frame," it is better to take this as an indication of how God views his opponent. We get a glimpse that what rightly terrifies Job is no terror at all to God. As God surveys the monster with Job, he sounds anything but defensive or morose or apologetic. I cannot help but think that God sounds entirely calm and even joyful as he details the creature's "goodly frame:" "Look at those scales, Job! What claws, what fiery breath! Amazing! I cannot wait for the day I unsheathe my sword and end that evil."

This must have been revolutionary for Job. He already knew distantly about Leviathan (3:8) and did once speak about God's defeat of the twisting serpent (26:11–13). But Job did not know how to connect God's defeat of evil to his own predicament. Nor did he have any idea of the joy with which God would go to battle against the chaos at loose in his world.

We can look at it this way. When David does not so much as flinch before Goliath's threat, but trusts God for victory (1 Sam. 17:45–46), his courage is inspiring, to say the least. But when Jesus looks full upon the physical agonies of crucifixion and the spiritual agonies of his punishment as a substitute, and does so not just with courage but with *joy* (Heb. 12:2), we have moved into another world altogether. If you were following a general into battle who showed courage in the face of death, you might be roused to imitate him. But what if your great captain and warrior looked on a dreadful enemy with a calm, serene happiness? What if an enemy that could easily kill you could not diminish your captain's unruffled cheerfulness in battle? How would that make you look at the enemy differently? How would it transform the entire battlefield? Leviathan looks at spears and swords like straw (41:26), but God looks at Leviathan like straw. A single glimpse of that beast would bring us to our knees. But when we hear our divine warrior speaking of Leviathan's "goodly frame," everything looks different. Leviathan is still nothing but violence and turmoil, still overwhelmingly, unbearably fierce, unstoppably powerful to destroy, even to destroy our lives. But as God describes fang and muscle and scale and claw with serene joy, a curious result follows:

as our terror before Leviathan deepens, we simultaneously see God even more gloriously as a perfect Savior and friend. We see him ever more clearly as the only one able and happy to master the evil at loose in his world. And we rejoice as we sense his unflinching joy in the task. In other words, the longer the description of Leviathan goes on and the more terrifying the monster becomes, the more clearly we see the contrast to God as a perfect Savior, shepherd, warrior, friend, Redeemer, and whatever else we need. This text has been put together very carefully. The location of verse 12 before the long description of the monster in verses 13–34 is calculated gloriously to present God in unmatched mastery of a chaos that grows ever more hideous the more we see of it. Paradoxically, it is just in taking in the dismaying breadth of the monster's proportions that we really see God for the happy Savior that he is. The more frightening Leviathan becomes, the more we are able to appreciate the God who goes to battle for us—a God who is more able to save Job than Leviathan is able to destroy him.

None of this is explicit, of course. I am trying to follow the unequal comparison between God and Leviathan in 41:11, followed by the apparently praiseworthy way God speaks of the monster in verse 12, all with a view to appreciating Job's transformation from faithful but embittered protest to abject worship. Approaching the Leviathan speech with all this in mind, we see that the one person who most clearly sees everything wrong with his world is the one person in the debate between Job and his friends who views the world most joyfully. Who else could talk about the monster's "goodly frame"? Remember how Job saw the world as a violent inner-city ghetto (12:13–25; 24:1–17), and the friends saw God's world like a boarding school for troubled teens—at best, a chance to get your act together so that God does not clobber you (5:1–7). God's perspective on his world is completely different. He is the one person in the book of Job who views creation with unblinking realism and unmixed joy. Not even Leviathan can diminish God's joy in his world! But this is not because God has blinkers on that keep him from seeing the truth about his realm. We learn in chapter 41 that God is the one person who sees the monster up close. Job thought his suffering had revealed to him the ugly, horrible truth about living in God's world. The Leviathan speech not only shows Job that the world is (if I can put it this way) much worse than Job ever suspected, because Leviathan is far more fearsome than Job ever imagined. It also shows that God is far more joyful than Job ever suspected. The one person who sees the world perfectly is the most joyful about it. As a result, surely God's perspective counts for more than Job's? Surely there must be a way to look on the world, just as it is, before the redemption of all things, a world where cancer and divorce and abuse still happen—and rejoice with God?

None of this implies that Leviathan is somehow good from a higher perspective or is meant to blur the line between good and evil. Leviathan is nothing but terror from snout to tail. At the same time, God's perspective on his world as Creator has more weight than ours, for he sees the whole, whereof we see the part. And the joy with which heaven views creation (remember 38:7), a joy that not even Leviathan can diminish, surely means that we can engage with God's world in the same way, even as we are still vulnerable to suffering, even before the redemption of all things. Even when we enter a Job-like ordeal, we can rejoice.[12]

---

12 Behemoth as "the first of the works of God" in 40:19 may point in the same direction. The verse is a difficult one, but it may mean that Behemoth ranks highly with his Creator because one of the most important things God does is bring his sword near and slay the monster, all in order to save those who trust him.

Looked at this way, Job 41 is quite a dizzying passage. The world is both far worse and far better than we ever suspected. The chaos and evil that God tolerates (but only for a time) are far more frightening than we thought; if we could see it up close, we would have a hard time keeping our feet (41:9). But God's assurance of victory over that monster is far calmer and happier than we ever suspected. This does not make Leviathan any less frightening or the chaos it represents any less foreboding. Cancer and car accidents and human trafficking are still awful tragedies. None of us is entirely safe. But when God sees the whole of the world's evil of which we get only a glimpse, and he speaks of his future victory with a calm joy, we too can engage with God's sometimes dangerous world not just with courage but with joy and peace. God is not intimidated one iota by the evil that could easily swallow us—so we do not need to be either.

God's joy in his survey of Leviathan becomes even more poignant when we remember that it took the death of God's precious Son to redeem the world, and that only in the crucifixion are those rebellious spiritual powers disarmed and led captive (Col. 2:15). God's utterly realistic joy in his world before the redemption of all things is already a profound and moving thing. But when we consider that it required the ultimate sacrifice for God to redeem his creation and defeat Leviathan, and that God rejoices in his world regardless of the suffering it will cost his Son, what then? Were God to give his Son grudgingly, we would still be duty bound to praise and thank him every day for a gift we could never deserve or pay him back for. But when God looks on his world joyfully with Job, knowing what it will cost him to bring the promise of 41:7–8 true—words fail us. What profound graciousness, what profound joy must emanate from even the heart of heaven over God's broken world!

What Have We Learned?

1. When God allows us or a Christian friend to suffer in some terrible and extreme way—when we look at our life and cannot but conclude that we have solid evidence that God does not love us—when we are tempted to draw terrible new conclusions about God's character in light of our suffering—Job 40–41 speaks to us powerfully and directly.

2. The world is worse than we know. There is a sinister power at work in the world of which we are at best dimly aware, which would terrify us if we could see it up close.

3. God tolerates this evil only for now. He keeps it on a tight leash (remember 38:10–11) and promises to defeat it gloriously one day. At the end of all time, God is going to give those who persevere with a faith like Job's a front-row seat as he goes to battle against an enemy we can barely comprehend in a conflict too awesome for words. Evil is only a temporary intruder in God's world, suffering only a temporary break in God's goodness to us. He promises us he will redeem all things, and all shall be well, and all manner of thing shall be well.

4. When we are undergoing intense suffering, it can be tempting to think that God asks too much of us—that living in God's world is too high a price to pay. When these thoughts occur to us, it is helpful to remember that the price is far higher for the Son of God. Both our earthly lives and eternal life are gifts given us by God through his Son. But if journeying through our earthly lives involves at times overwhelming pain, it

involves far deeper agony for the Son of God. Our sufferings are small indeed compared to Christ's, but God keeps giving his world another sunrise, heedless of what it costs him, and does so happily.

5. What would it be to view God's world with utter realism about that dark and sinister chaos at work behind the visible fabric of things, while simultaneously rejoicing with God in his world today, before the redemption of all things?

Job's Worship and Restoration

(Job 42)

THROUGHOUT THE BOOK OF JOB, we have seen the steadfastness of God's servant in his suffering. Although Job has said some deeply foolish things about God, he never cuts off his relationship with God but instead speaks repeatedly of his desire to meet with God and reconcile. Job has responded appropriately to God's first speech, admitting his protest was wrong, but he does not say much more beyond that. Now Job has seen Leviathan up close and heard about God's coming victory over the monster. He has learned that Leviathan is more fearsome than he imagined and the divine warrior more joyful than he ever suspected. How will Job respond?

"Now My Eye Sees You": Job's Profound Worship (42:1–6)

In some of the most moving words in all of Scripture, we see Job's earlier guarded response (40:3–5) break into abject worship and total comfort in God. "I know that you can do all things, and that no purpose of yours can be thwarted" (42:2). Job isn't speaking of

God's power in a general sense; rather, he is expressing new assurance and comfort that God's good purposes for him can never be thwarted—not even by as fearsome a power as Leviathan. God means Job only good, even in the midst of unimaginable loss, and nothing can stop God's purposes for Job. "Therefore I have uttered what I did not understand" (42:3)—Job realizes how profoundly foolish it was to cast God in the role of enemy and torturer, when God is a great warrior and Savior for Job against an evil Job can barely imagine. "All those criticisms I uttered against you—I had no idea what I was talking about! You've been my truest friend all along!"

Job also happily confesses he's been caught up in wonders too great for him (42:3). The word *wonders* is often used to describe those great acts of salvation accomplished by God to rescue his helpless people (see Ex. 3:20; Josh. 3:5; Pss. 72:18; 77:12; 86:10; 98:1; 131:1; 136:4; and so on). Job uses this word to express his happy submission and reconciliation to the God working saving wonders on his behalf.

In 42:4–5, Job makes an interesting leap that, along with verses 2–3, shows his new blessed state before God. Job quotes God's initial question from 38:3 and 40:7 but instead of answering any of the specific questions that God previously asked about the sunrise or the ocean or the raven, he says only, "Now my eye sees you." It is as if Job is saying, "You want an answer, Lord? All I can say to your questions is, now I see who you really are. I see you for the faithful friend and powerful ally and warrior I need, and rest content." Job also draws a contrast between his new insight and all his former knowledge of God, which was not slight (see 1:1). He relegates all his former knowledge of God to mere hearsay and secondhand rumor ("the hearing of the ear"). Job knows who God is far more intimately now, to his profound comfort.

In light of his new knowledge of God, Job goes far beyond merely withdrawing his protest, as he did in 40:3–5. He heartily despises himself for ever having suggested that God is malicious or distant or uncaring (42:6). He also simultaneously repents and expresses his absolute comfort in the midst of his losses in verse 6. I say "simultaneously" because the verb that Job uses at the end of 42:6 can be translated either as "repent" or "be comforted," such that Job might be saying that he either repents in dust and ashes or is comforted about dust and ashes. Either translation fits so well that I suspect the double entendre is intentional. I also suspect that "dust and ashes" means two things simultaneously: the phrase expresses Job's profound humility in repenting and also refers symbolically to Job's suffering. The same phrase is used in 30:19 to describe Job's agony; and remember that Job is sitting on the ash heap as he says this (2:7). All this means that Job is doing far more than withdrawing his protest, as he did at the end of God's first speech. Job is both humbly repenting of his former criticisms of God and also confessing that he is entirely comforted in God over all his former losses. His dead children, his physical pain, his alienation from his wife, the barbs from his faithless friends—Job had formerly found all this unbearable. But his terrible losses are now swallowed up in God.[1]

What is amazing about this passage is that Job expresses his utter comfort in God *before* he is restored. Job's restoration does not begin until 42:10. In 42:6, he is still on the ash heap, still casting sidelong glances at the graves of his children, still covered in sores. Before Job's life changes back into one of blessing, however, Job is utterly and entirely comforted in God alone.

1 As John Walton puts it, what satisfies Job at the end of the book is not an explanation but knowing God better. *Job*, NIV Application Commentary (Grand Rapids, MI: Eerdmans, 2012), 342.

God is able to do the same for you. We will soon see how God's intention for his children is blessing in both our earthly and spiritual lives and that times of suffering are only temporary interruptions that God always eventually heals. This is a wonderful truth that we should cling to when God does allow us to suffer. But suffering Christians are not restricted merely to waiting for some happy future. God is able to draw near to you as a perfect and all-sufficient Savior and warrior and friend, utterly to comfort you, while you are still on the ash heap.

God does not love Job more than he loves you—even if your level of spirituality does not match Job's, you are under the same friendship and divine favor that Job enjoyed. And even if God does not literally appear to you in the storm as he did to Job, he is nonetheless able and even happy to draw near to you and speak gently but directly into your torment, so that, like Job, you are able to say from your roots, "Now I see who you really are, and I am utterly comforted."

Job's joy and comfort in God become even more moving when we remember that Job never received any explanation as to why the tragedy of chapters 1–2 happened. He has had his eyes opened to a greater spiritual conflict and been assured God is not his enemy. But he never learns what the reader does in chapter 1 about the terrible necessity of demonstrating that Job loves God without ulterior motive (1:9, 21). It must be this way, however: if God were ever to reveal to Job the devil's accusation, the accuser could claim Job remained faithful because he knew God would restore him after Job said the right thing. An essential part of a Job-like ordeal is permanent ignorance, that maddening sense that far more is going on than we can grasp. God's comforting and restoration of Job, profound and beautiful as it is, does not bring with it any explanations for Job. Job goes to his grave never understanding why his ordeal occurred.

Job's Vindication (42:7–9)

The book of Job, along with the rest of Scripture, shows that God's policy toward his children is one of generosity even in earthly matters, and that times of suffering are only temporary exceptions. Before Job is lifted out of the ash heap and restored to life and blessing, however, another matter must be resolved. God is terribly angry with Job's friends, and his anger will only break after Job sacrifices for them and intercedes on their behalf (42:8–9). In fact, the depth of God's anger at the false accusations of the friends can be gauged by the fact that normally one animal is sufficient to secure atonement (see Lev. 1–7). The friends must offer seven!

How we speak to each other matters deeply to God. These verses encourage those undergoing a Job-like ordeal and smarting under the well-intentioned but deeply wounding words of other Christians, for God will similarly vindicate modern-day Jobs who suffer suspicion and accusation from false friends. They also caution those of us who might be quick to give advice to sufferers that only hurts—those among us who might overestimate our ability to understand what our friends are going through and try to "fix" them in a way that deepens their pain.

Note as well how God's anger toward and restoration of the friends break their theology. According to their thinking, sin always leads to punishment. In this case, however, God forgives them because of the intercession of their better, not because they reform their lives and clean themselves up before God. Note as well that God wants Job's self-righteous friends restored, and takes the initiative to make sure that Job's friends can reenter God's favor, all before they repent. By the same token, asking Job to pray for them clearly humbles them before Job while also preventing any lingering resentment on Job's part against his friends. God wants no more anger, suspicion, and attacks between the participants in the debate. But he settles the argument in a way that vindicates Job and demonstrates that he is far kinder to sinners than the friends ever suspected.

The shocking thing about this passage is, of course, that the basis of God's anger is that the friends have not spoken rightly about him, as Job has (42:7). Given Job's extended and passionate protests against God, this is quite a surprise! This cannot be a carte blanche approval of everything Job has said, however, because God says this only after Job repents of his protests. Not even Job approves of everything he said during the course of the debate. At the same time, we have also seen throughout how, even when Job protests, his theology remains remarkably good; even in the midst of his protest, he still thought of God as all-powerful and all-knowing (9:2–19; 12:13) and still confessed that without God's friendship, he saw no point to being alive at all (chap. 3). Remember as well how Job did not know how to think about himself outside of God's approval of him (9:21). The only mistake Job makes has to do with God's heart toward him, and even as Job makes this mistake, he refuses to sever his relationship with the God whom he thinks hates him.[2]

I am not trying to lessen the shock of this verse (42:7). We see God's astounding kindness to Job here, giving Job (as it were) as much credit as possible, not lashing back at him for his criticisms but treating him graciously. We also see the way in which God sweetens Job's restoration by mixing gentle challenges of Job's unworthy theol-

2 I have tried to explore more deeply how Job spoke rightly about God in my article "How Did Job Speak Rightly about God?" *Themelios* 43 (2018): 350–58.

ogy with extremely gracious reception of Job's imperfect but genuine faithfulness. God's restoration of modern-day Jobs is no less kind.

Job's Restoration (42:10–17)

The poetry of the book of Job is so intense, and the debate between the friends continues at such length, that the reader can leave the book with the feeling that Job's nightmare is the deepest truth of his existence and his time of blessing at the beginning and end an exception. The opposite is the case, however. The book of Job shows us that those times when God makes a tragic but necessary exception to his kindness to us are always temporary—God's consistent policy toward us is blessing and *shalom* in both our spiritual and earthly lives. This policy is interrupted only to seal us in a genuine relationship with God (1:21) that will preserve us in God's joy in eternity and allow us to enjoy earthly blessings without them corrupting that deeper spiritual relationship.

"And the LORD restored the fortunes of Job" (42:10). Job has proved beyond any doubt that he loves God simply for God's sake, regardless of what earthly blessings are given to him or taken away. As a result, there is no reason for the ordeal to continue, and God's normal policy of goodness can be reinstated. The nightmare recedes into the past as Job's family succeeds where his friends failed by actually comforting him (42:11; see 2:11). Instead of giving Job long, moralistic speeches, their financial gifts are a means of showing honor to Job and helping him rebuild his ruined estate.[3] Job's family helps in practical ways, not by preaching at him.

---

3 See John Hartley, *The Book of Job*, New International Commentary on the Old Testament (Grand Rapids, MI: Eerdmans, 1988), 541; and Bruce Waltke, *An Old Testament Theology: An Exegetical, Canonical, and Thematic Approach* (Grand Rapids, MI: Zondervan, 2007), 945.

The Lord does more than just get Job back to where he was. Job's latter end is twice as beautiful as his beginning (42:12–14). Infant mortality rates in the ancient world were tragically high,[4] so holding one's grandchildren would have been blessing enough—but Job was able to enjoy great-grandchildren. This is a biblical way of saying that Job enjoyed a fairy-tale level of blessing after his trial. God allowed Job to suffer in about every way possible during his ordeal. Now he withholds no blessing that is his to give.

That Job gives his daughters an inheritance along with his sons is a small but significant detail (42:15). Normal practice in this culture was to have inheritance run through the male line (see Num. 27; 36), which meant that women were financially dependent on their husbands. As a result, widows in biblical times could be terribly vulnerable financially. Although there may have been some inheritance from their dead husband (as in Ruth 4:3), or they may have been able to marry another member from among their in-laws (Deut. 25:5–10), levirate marriage was not a requirement, and poor husbands might leave their wives destitute. This means that when Job includes his daughters in his inheritance, he is planning ahead to provide for his daughters in case tragedy strikes and they suffer widowhood. Job understands God's plan for his world is sometimes to allow terrible suffering—but instead of protesting against this, Job does what he can to help (potential) widows and orphans in his midst. This, in turn, prompts us to ask how we can help those suffering around us in practical ways. In the end, the book of Job intends to make us not only wiser in suffering but also more active on behalf of the helpless (James 1:27).

4   Estimates range between 50–70 percent of children in the biblical world dying either in childbirth or infancy. See Carol Meyers, *Rediscovering Eve: Ancient Israelite Women in Context* (Oxford, UK: Oxford University Press, 2013), 110.

"And so Job died, an old man, and full of days" (42:17). The last verse of this long and challenging book is deeply poignant as a great saint comes to the end of his life. Job steadfastly endured under trial, and God restored him (James 5:11). But what was it like for Job when he stood before God in eternity? When the great Redeemer who had spoken to him from the storm finally spoke to him face-to-face?

What Have We Learned?

1. Job-like ordeals are awful, but they are always temporary—a tragically necessary exception in God's normal policy of generosity toward his earthly children in matters both spiritual and temporal. As the genuineness of the saint's faith and love in God is proved, God restores that saint to blessing and shalom in their earthly lives. Every Job-like ordeal has, in God's providence, a happy ending of perfect restoration.

2. God is able to draw near to sufferers and gloriously comfort them with his own person, all before their losses are restored and their sufferings erased. God can utterly and fully comfort a modern-day Job simply out of his own person, so that, like Job, we say, "Now my eye sees you."

3. One part of the restoration of a modern-day Job involves the vindication of that sufferer in relation to other believers who tried to help but only hurt. If you have been hurt by other Christians who blamed you when they should have listened, your restoration to intimacy with God will also involve God vindicating you in relation to those Christians who condemned you.

4. God's restoring work is meant to make us more alert and active in helping those sufferers in our midst. Just as Job counteracts normal custom by setting aside inheritances for his daughters, so restored sufferers should be especially sensitive to suffering around them, not presuming to be able to act as a Savior for anyone else, but also not passive.

Concluding Reflections

THIS BOOK IS INTENDED to help Christians suffer well by being wise about suffering. Endurance in suffering involves more than discernment, of course. But awareness of the Bible's portrayal of the different kinds of trials that God allows is one crucial part of enduring with joy in the midst of pain. In the first chapter of this book, we considered different sorts of ordeals that Christians undergo and explored what promises God makes in each, as well as considering what he expects from us in each. Against this background, we have spent most of our time on one distinct sort of ordeal that is less well understood, in which God allows pain that is both intense and inexplicable. We have seen how a Job-like ordeal has nothing to do with any punishment for sin or with spiritual growth. It rather demonstrates the sincerity of our love for God himself and not just his gifts. Indeed, we have seen that the tear-stained confessions we make when God allows tragedy, and we bless his name regardless (1:21), not only prove the reality of our relationship with God but seal us in it. When we echo Job's confession, we receive the outcome of our faith and are able to see God as God and Lord in a whole new way.

This means that Job-like suffering is, in God's hands, his way of fitting us for eternity. The book of Job warns us ahead of time that God will occasionally allow us to suffer to such a degree that we seriously wonder if God loves us at all. God will give us every earthly reason to give up on him, putting us in a position where all our confessions of faith stop being theoretical and gain a terrible weight. There is a sense, however, in which God must do so, because a relationship with God where a saint can repeat Job 1:21 not only in safety and comfort but also in the midst of terrible pain is the only kind of relationship with God that will save us.

We have also seen how, despite the magnitude of Job's suffering and its terrible perplexity, God's requirement of us in the midst of a Job-like ordeal is actually very simple: God wants us to maintain our relationship with him. His only expectation is that we not break faith with him and walk away. He does not expect a Zen-like calm. Although God does challenge Job's protests against him, we have seen God's extraordinary gentleness with Job in his protests.

We have also considered how God's restoration of a saint from a Job-like ordeal does not involve explanations. One part of a Job-like ordeal is a maddening sense that more is happening to you than you can understand. God's restoration of Job, although perfectly comforting a man who had lost everything (42:6), does not relieve Job's sense of perplexity. An essential element of a Job-like ordeal is permanent ignorance.

We have also considered at length God's great promise of Leviathan's defeat. God shows Job in terrible detail the chaos in his creation that he tolerates, but only for a time. God thus assures Job that he is not Job's enemy, that he is far more aware of what is wrong with his world than Job is, and that there is coming a day when he will slay the monster, and all things shall be made new.

Furthermore, we have seen how every Job-like ordeal ends in comfort and restoration. No matter how nightmarish the suffering,

God does not allow it to continue forever. We have also seen how God draws near to Job in a way that perfectly comforts him before anything in his life improves.

We have also considered the joy that permeates God's speeches, and if there is anything that the reader remembers from this book, I hope it is this. We have seen how, out of all the characters in the book of Job and their perspectives on creation, God is the one person who is both the most realistic about the supernatural chaos and evil still active in his world and also the one person happiest in his world, before the defeat of Leviathan and the redemption of all things. If the one person who sees Leviathan up close views creation this way, then surely it must be possible for those who trust God to do as well? And if the one person who must make the greatest sacrifice imaginable in order for creation to be redeemed is still happy for the sun to rise each morning, then surely it must be possible to look squarely at our worst nightmares and rejoice with God? What would it be for those who echo Job's faith (1:21) to be utterly realistic about the world—we who, like Job, have seen Leviathan up close through the poetry of chapter 41—while also joyfully waiting on God's final victory over all evil and suffering? If the sons of God burst into song when God made the world, will we remain silent? If God can look on Leviathan with serene calm (41:10–12), what courage and joy can be ours as we engage with our lives, knowing Leviathan is still active but his destruction is coming?

General Index

abomination, 79
absence of God, 26
accuser, 39–41, 44, 45, 48, 50–51,
    53–56, 69, 74, 79, 90, 168
angels, singing at the sight of God's
    world, 134
animals, God's care for, 134–35
Anthony, Lawrence, 138
ash heap, 55–56, 64, 167

Baal, 153
Behemoth, 119, 141, 146–48; as "first
    of the works of God," 161n12; as
    symbolic, 154n11
"Be Still My Soul" (hymn), 46–47
Bildad, 62, 81, 97
black holes, 137–38
blaming the sufferer, 75–77, 86–87
blessing: for faithfulness, 131; God's
    intention for his children, 168,
    171; in the Old Testament, 53

chaos, 97, 121, 129, 177; defeat of,
    152, 156–58; exists only at God's
    permission, 39, 58, 135–36;
    limiting of, 130; tolerated only for
    a time, 162, 176
Christian life, reflects Israel's history,
    23–24

Christlikeness, 22
confession of sin, 29, 78–79
counsel, 122
creation, 125–28; as a building, 126;
    goodness of, 126; moral edge to,
    131–32; tour of, 119, 132
Creator-creature distinction, 154
crocodile, 150–51
cursing in the Old Testament, 41, 53

Daniel, prayers of, 18
David: and Goliath, 159; lament of,
    28–29, 33; mourns his sin, 17;
    persecution of, 21
death, 109
desert-like experience, 24–27
devil, 39n4. See also accuser
discernment, in trials, 15
disorder, in God's world, 130
divine warrior, 143, 145, 159, 165,
    166
dreams, 67; "dust and ashes," 167

Egypt, Israel's craving for, 26
elephant, 138, 139
Elihu, 82–84, 112
Eliphaz, 62; attempt to comfort
    himself, 75–77; failed to say
    anything helpful or healing, 96;

first speech, 64–69; moralism of, 80; as mouthpiece for the devil, 68; second speech, 71; superficial plausibility of, 80; theology of, 70–72
endurance in suffering, 175
evil. *See* chaos
evildoers, 81, 82, 129, 146
exile, 20

faithfulness, brings large harvests and military victory, 131
faith and works, 37
fear of God, 36, 64, 65
Fine, Cordelia, 76–77
friend, withholding kindness from, 78
friendship with God, 36, 38
friendship with modern-day sufferers, 91
friends of Job, 56–57; condemnation from, 85; distance of God in later speeches, 74; failure to help Job, 96, 112; God's anger and restoration of, 169–70; as his tormenters, 63; retribution theology of, 124; self-righteousness of, 85

God: allows chaos and evil in his world, 130, 153, 156; allows for predators in the animal world, 134–35, 136, 142; allows for suffering, 136, 142; all-sufficiency of, 46, 58; appearance in the storm, 121, 145; becomes strange to Job, 57; can feel inaccessible in suffering, 117; care for creation, 128, 134–35; "diapers" the sea, 129–30; did not create evil, 154n11; draws near and comforts sufferers, 116, 173; first speech of, 119–42; generosity of, 169; gentleness of, 122–24, 142, 176; goes to war against great powers, 121, 160; goodness of, 114, 126, 128; as great condemner, 68–69;

incomprehensibility of, 140; justice of, 84, 132, 139, 144, 146, 154, 157; and Leviathan, 149–50; love and commendation toward Job, 41; not angry with Job, 136–37; restoration of those who suffer, 88; as perfect Savior and shepherd, 160; proud of Job, 41, 59, 124n2; providence of, 53n10, 50–54, 58; questions Job on the founding of the earth, 125–28; second speech of, 121, 143–55; sees true dimensions of Job's suffering, 156; silence of, 83–84; sovereignty of, 50–51, 58, 113; transcendence and greatness of, 98; victory over chaos and evil, 156–58, 162; wisdom of, 113, 151
God-forsakenness, 27–30
goodness of God's world, 126, 134
grace, 47, 52, 67, 68, 158

hawk, 132, 134, 139
heavenly courtroom, 38, 51
hell, 56
helpless, active in behalf of, 172
hippopotamus, 150–51
hope, 15, 30, 102–11, 112
"how long," 30
human psychology, 75
human smallness, false equation with moral fault, 81
humility: first step in wisdom, 142; in speaking to others, 81

idolatry and unrighteousness, bring military defeat and famine, 131
inexplicable suffering, 31–33, 50, 61, 63
infant mortality in the ancient world, 172
intimacy with God, 27, 29, 46, 48, 95, 98

Inuit, 138
Israel, wilderness wandering of, 22–27

Jesus Christ: death redeems the world,
162; entered into Job's suffering,
114–16, 117; joy in the physical
agonies of crucifixion, 159; suffering of, 163–64
Job: as blameless, 36, 101–2; blesses
God when Got takes away, 52–53;
close to death, 55, 57, 65–66,
109; comforted in God over
all former losses, 166, 167–68;
contradictions in speeches, 105,
111; curse on creation, 64, 93,
96; curses his own existence,
93, 96; death of, 173; desire for
death, 105; despair of, 102; does
not curse God, 102–3; exemplary
in obedience, 47; fearing God
"without cause," 55n11; to gird
up his loins, 124, 143; hope for
reconciliation, 102, 107, 112;
includes daughters in his inheritance, 172, 174; innocence of, 73,
144; intercession for friends,
169–70; interpretation of his
suffering, 144; joyously reunited
with God, 109, 110; limited perspective of, 97, 99, 126, 132–33;
love for God, 114; low point, 97,
99, 101; new knowledge of God,
166–67; "none like him on the
earth," 40; obscuring counsel of
God, 122; personal integrity in
the midst of his ordeal, 101, 103,
112, 114; picture-perfect life,
36; protest against God, 96–102,
111, 136–37, 141; repentance
and comfort of, 167; restoration
of, 167, 176–77; seeks to be right
with God, 97–98; self-imprecation, 111; shadowy anticipation

of Christ, 92, 114–16; theology
changes little in his suffering,
113–14; unfamiliarity to Christians, 12; vindication of, 169–70;
widening perspective of, 144;
worship of God, 120, 141, 143,
150–52, 160, 165–66
Job (book): difficult and wearying
length of, 91; poetry of, 91, 92,
93, 94, 114, 137
Job-like ordeal" always temporary, 173;
and permanent perplexity, 176;
fits us for eternity, 175; inexpli-
cability of, 90; peculiar dignity to
it, 117; poetry describes it from
the inside, 114; speaking to, 85;
uniqueness of, 47–50, 57
Joseph, suffering of, 20
joy, 13, 127; in creation, 161; permeates God's speeches, 177
judgment on the wicked, 70
justice, 149n4

kinsman-redeemer, 107

lament, 27–30, 32, 89
Leviathan, 119, 121, 141, 146–47,
165, 166; as chaos monster,
153–55; defeat of, 176, 177;
"goodly frame" of, 158–60; no
comparison with God, 160; as
symbolic, 154n11
levirate marriage, 172
Lewis, C. S., 43–44, 139–40
light, 127
lion, 134, 139
listening to Job, 100
love of neighbor, 77
loving God for his own sake, 42–45,
48, 58
"lying down" in the dust, 109n5

mantis shrimp, 138, 139
mediator, 84, 106–9

Merton, Thomas, 43
misremembering, 26
monsters, symbols of chaos and evil, 121
moralism, ugliness of, 79–80

Nehemiah, prayers of, 18
new covenant benefits, 42

obedience, 36, 37, 52
ocean, 166
old covenant blessings, 42
order and goodness of God's world, 134
ordinary animals, 152, 154
ostrich, 133, 139, 141
Owen, John, 21

pain, distorts our view of the world, 133, 142
"patient listening" with Job, 91
persecution, for Christ's sake, 21–22
personal integrity, 36, 64, 65
pilgrimage, 24–25
"plural of majesty," 151
preservation of the saints, 53n10
problem of evil, 39, 141
providence, 53n10, 50–54, 58
psalms of lament, 26, 28–29, 90

raven, 134, 139, 166
realism, 136, 164
Redeemer, 107–11
redemption, 94, 95, 108, 161–62, 166
rejoicing over God's creation, 127, 164
religious psychology, 75
repentance, 19, 48–49, 70, 97, 167
resurrection, 106, 109n5, 110
retribution principle, 37, 52, 66, 68, 74, 124; as general and long-term principle, 71–72; narrow and automatic version, 71–72, 75, 80
"rising above the dust," 108–9

Satan, 39–40n4
sea: "diapering" of, 128–30; rebellious-ness of, 129–30; symbol of chaos, 97, 121, 129
secondary blessings, 41, 42, 45, 74, 79, 95
self-righteousness, of friends of job, 85
seven (number), 36
shalom, 56, 79, 146, 171
Sheol, 95–96
sin, and suffering, 16–19, 156
Son of God, suffering of, 162, 163
"sons of God," 38–39
sowing and reaping, 68, 71
spiritual growth: through lament, 29–30; from suffering, 19–21
stoicism, 52
storms, in the Old Testament, 120–21
subatomic particles, 138
sufferer, vindication of, 173
suffering: as Christian calling, 11; ends in comfort and restoration, 176–77; and holding onto God, 49; inexplicableness of, 31–33, 50, 61, 63; of innocent, 74; as punish-ment, 81–82, 83–84; no quick or easy solution to, 117; no tight connection with sin, 156; only temporary, 168, 169; and repen-tance, 48–49; for sin, 16–19; and sovereignty and goodness of God, 39; and spiritual growth, 19–21
suffering friends: alertness in helping, 172, 174; and temptation to com-fort ourselves, 87; walking with, 86; will say crazy things in their pain, 87, 100
sunrise, 131–32, 137, 141, 166

Ten Commandments, 16, 17
Thessalonians, steadfastness amid perse-cution, 21
trauma, 86

uncleanness, 56, 79
undeserved suffering, 72
union with Christ, 48

Walton, John, 125n4, 149n4, 167n1
warhorse, 132, 137
wedding vows, 45–46
wicked, 146
widows and orphans, 172
wilderness wandering, 22–27
wisdom: distinguishes appearance
from reality, 80; and humility,

142; passed on through questions, 128n6; training in, 91,
115
wise speech, 61, 96
wonders, 166
world: as far better and far worse than
we imagine, 140, 162, 163; stability of, 126
worship, 28–29, 42, 53, 58
wrath of God, 57

Zophar, 62, 74, 81–82, 134

Scripture Index

Genesis
1 16
1:3 94
2 16
3 .... 154n11
26:24 40
29:17 147
37 20
37:9 .... 20n2
39:20 20
39:26–27 20
40–41 67
41:1 20
50:15–21 20
50:20 157

Exodus
3:20 166
6:6 145
14 25
14:31 40
15–17 .... 22, 24
15:16 145
15:22–24 25
15:26–27 25
16:3 25
16:12–13 24
16:21 24

16:22–30 24
16:31 26
19:16 27
20:10 134
20:19 27
24:11 110
28:3 113
31:3 113
31:6 113

Leviticus
1–7 169
11:13–19 134
13:18–20 56
17:10–12 134
18:21–25 79
25:25–28 107
25:35–46 107
26 .... 37, 42,
          131

Numbers
10 26
11–14 .... 22, 24
11:4 26
11:4–6 26
11:5 26
11:6 26
11:7–9 26

13–14 23
16:13 26
17:25 39
24:4 110
24:16 110
27 172
36 172

Deuteronomy
4:12 27
8:2–5 23
10:12–16 36
19:15–16 108
25:5–10 172
28 .... 37, 42,
          131
28:27 55
28:35 55

Joshua
3:5 166

Ruth
4:1–12 107
4:3 172

1 Samuel
2:7–8 71
10:24 .... 40n6

16:12.........147
17:45–46 159
17:55.........123n2
20:31.........39
29:4 ....40n4

2 Samuel
7:5............40
12:17.........17
13:19.........56
15:31.........122
16:20.........122
19:23.........40n4

1 Kings
1:12 122
3:12 ....40n6
8:23 40
18:24.........51
21............72
22............38

2 Kings
1:12 51
14:23–27 72
17:7–23......17
18:5 ....40n6
23:35.........40n6
25:1–21......17

2 Chronicles
7:1............51
10:13.........122

Nehemiah
9.............18

Esther
4:1............56

Job
1–2..........47, 57, 59,
            63, 64,
            64n2, 66,

68, 70, 73,
79, 82, 97,
99, 101,
103, 104,
108, 126,
144, 168
1:1............36, 37, 47,
            68, 166
1:1–5.........35–38
1:2–3.........50, 52
1:2–5.........36, 37, 41
1:3............36
1:4............36
1:5............36
1:6–12 ....38–50, 54
1:6–7.........39
1:8............40, 41, 47,
            52, 59, 68,
            85, 114,
            116
1:9............41, 43, 50,
            74, 79,
            168
1:11 ....41, 53
1:12 ....40n4, 44,
            45, 50, 51
1:13–19......50–52, 53
1:15 51
1:17 51
1:20–21......52
1:20–22......52–54
1:21 ....40, 44, 52,
            53, 54, 57,
            67, 69, 95,
            168, 171,
            175, 176,
            177
2:1–3.........44
2:1–10 54–56
2:2............44
2:3............54
2:4............109
2:4–5.........55

2:6............55
2:7............65, 109,
            167
2:7–8.........55
2:8............56, 147
2:9............56, 69
2:10 ....56, 57
2:11 ....75, 171
2:11–13......56–57
2:12 ....57, 75
2:12–13......92
2:13 ....57, 93
3............64, 93,
            102
3:3............93
3:3–10 127
3:3–4.........94
3:4............93, 94
3:5............94
3:6............93
3:8............121, 148,
            155, 159
3:9–10 95
3:11 95
3:11–23......105
3:13 95
3:17 146
3:17–19......96
3:19 95
4............64–69
4–5..........71, 73, 81
4:2............64
4:3–4.........64, 65, 94
4:3–6.........64
4:5............64
4:6............64, 65
4:7............65, 66
4:8............66, 68, 69,
            71
4:9–11 66
4:11–12......69
4:11–21......66
4:12–16......66

4:13 67
4:14 67
4:15 67
4:17 67
4:17–21 66
4:18 68
4:18–21 68
4:19–21 68
5 70–73
5:1–7 .... 70, 160
5:2 70
5:4 70
5:8 70
5:8–9 71
5:9 71
5:10 71
5:11 71
5:11–14 70
5:12 144
5:15–16 70
5:17 70
5:18–26 78
5:18–27 70
5:19–26 70
5:23–25 79
6:4 96
6:10 73
6:14 78
6:15–20 96
6:15–27 96
6:21 75
6:25 63
6:27 77
6:28–30 73
7 96
7:5 109
7:7 .... 33, 113
7:12 .... 97, 121,
          136, 144
7:17–18 97
7:20 97
7:20–21 33

7:21 .... 97, 105,
          108,
          109n5
8:4 81
8:5 97
8:5–7 .... 78, 81
8:20 81
8:21 79
8:21–22 81
8:22 .... 81, 146
9–10 .... 97, 101
9:2 .... 97, 123n2
9:2–19 170
9:2–20 149
9:3 .... 98, 123
9:3–19 113
9:5–10 134
9:15 98
9:16 98
9:17 99
9:17–20 123
9:20 98
9:21 .... 101, 170
9:22–24 ...... 33, 99,
          103, 105,
          122, 129
9:23 99
9:24 .... 99, 100
9:25–26 100
9:27–10:4 ... 100
10:2 100
10:2–8 33
10:4–7 .... 100, 113
10:8–12 100
10:8–13 ...... 95, 100,
          113
10:11 96
10:13 100
10:14–17 100
10:15 101
10:18 .... 102, 113
10:18–22 100
10:20 102

10:20–22 105
10:21–22 102
11:5–6 124
11:5–11 82
11:5–12 134
11:6 82
11:7–8 82
11:12–23 82
11:13 82
11:13–19 78
11:17 79
11:20 146
11:22–31 82
12:7–9 139
12:12 82
12:13 .... 113, 170
13:13–14 104
13:13–23 103
12:13–25 .... 100, 114,
          160
13:15 .... 104, 116,
          140
13:15–16 73
13:16 105
13:18 104
13:20–21 104
13:22 .... 106, 124
13:23 103
13:24 103
13:24–27 106
13:28 106
14 106
14:1–6 106
14:7 106
14:7–9 106
14:8 108
14:12 .... 109n5
14:18–19 106
14:18–22 106
14:19 108
15 70
15:4 .... 73, 96,
          144

15:14–16 79
15:15 79
15:16 79
15:17–35 71
15:20 71
15:21 74
15:25 74
15:32 71
16 106
16:6 100
16:7–17 106
16:7–19 123
16:8 108
16:9–17 ...... 96, 135,
    144
16:18 107
16:18–22 84
16:19 107
16:21 107
16:22 107
17 106
17:13–16 105
17:16 108
19 .... 106, 111
19:5–12 100
19:7–12 106
19:13 108,
    108n3
19:13–19 107
19:15 108,
    108n3
19:23–24 107
19:23–27 55
19:25 107,
    108n4,
    109
19:25–27 .... 84, 108
19:26 110
19:26–27 .... 109, 110
19:27 108,
    108n3,
    110

20:11 108,
    109n5
20:15 74
20:26 108
20:28–29 74
21:7–33 100
21:26 .... 109n5
22 70
22:5 73
22:5–11 ...... 72, 75
23:3 84
23:3–6 140
23:3–7 105
23:8–9 .... 84, 117
23:13–17 33
24:1 .... 100, 122,
    155
24:1–17 ...... 129, 160
25 81
26:11–13 .... 121, 159
27:5–6 101
28:2 108
29 111
29:2–4 112
29:8–10 ...... 36, 37
29:11–17 37
29:16 37
30:19 167
31 111
31:6 112
31:16–23 37
31:31–34 37
31:33–34 .... 47, 67
31:40 112
32–37 83
32:2 83
32:3 83
32:6–7 82
32:14 83
33 83
33:13–19 84
33:14 84
33:19–22 84

33:23–25 84
33:26–27 84
3–31 57
3–37 .... 35, 61–88,
    120
34:15 108
35:9–11 84
35:12 129
35:12–15 84
36:5–16 84
36:7 84
36:8–9 84
36:10 84
36:11 84
36:12–14 84
38 .... 127n5
38–39 .... 127, 132,
    134, 137,
    139, 141,
    142, 146,
    157
38–41 .... 35, 123
38:1 .... 121, 122,
    145
38:1–3 120–25
38:2 .... 122, 124,
    130
38:2–3 125
38:3 .... 124, 143,
    166
38:4 .... 126, 128
38:4–7 80,
    125–28,
    133
38:4–38 119
38:5 .... 125, 126,
    127, 128
38:6 .... 125, 126
38:7 .... 127, 134,
    161
38:8–11 128–30,
    134
38:9 129

38:9–11......135
38:10–11....129, 163
38:11.........129
38:12.........132, 157
38:12–15....130–32
38:13.........131, 146
38:14.........137
38:15.........131
38:16–18....132
38:16–24....133
38:17.........137
38:19–21....132
38:25–27....134
38:25–28....157
38:31–33....132
38:34–35....135
38:39–39:30.119
38:39–40....135
38:39–41....132
39.............139, 153
39:1–4.......132
39:5–8.......132
39:9–12......132
39:13–18....132, 133
39:19–22....137
39:19–25....132, 135
39:26–30....132, 134
39:39–40....134
39:41.........134
40–41.........150, 152,
            153, 163
40:3–5.......120,
            140–41,
            149, 151,
            165, 167
40:7..........166
40:7–8.......143, 145,
            152
40:8..........144, 146,
            149,
            149n4,
            151, 154,
            157

40:8–14......143
40:8–9.......152
40:9–10......145, 152
40:9–14......145
40:10.........145, 146
40:11–13....146
40:12.........145, 146
40:13.........108, 145
40:15.........147, 151,
            152,
            154n11
40:15–24....119, 143,
            146
40:17.........154n11
40:17–18....147
40:19.........147, 152,
            156,
            161n12
40:20.........147
40:21–22....147
40:23.........147
40:24.........147, 152
40:25–29....152
41.............161
41:1–2.......148
41:1–7.......152
41:1–11......158
41:1–34......119, 143,
            146
41:3–4.......148
41:5–6.......148
41:7..........152
41:7–8.......121, 148,
            156, 157,
            162
41:9..........148, 156,
            162
41:10.........149, 155,
            157
41:10–12....177
41:11.........160
41:12.........158, 160
41:13–34....158, 160

41:15–17....148
41:18.........148
41:18–21....148,
            154n11
41:22.........148
41:26.........159
41:26–28....148
41:31–32....154n11
41:32–33....148
41:33.........152
42:1–6.......13, 35,
            120, 141,
            143, 151,
            155,
            165–69
42:2..........165
42:2–3.......166
42:3..........166
42:4–5.......166
42:5..........13, 40, 46,
            48, 49
42:5–6.......34, 86,
            105
42:6..........58, 90,
            167, 176
42:7..........170
42:7–8.......78, 87
42:7–9.......169–71
42:7–17......13, 35
42:8..........61
42:8–9.......169
42:10.........167
42:10–17....71,
            171–73
42:11.........51, 171
42:12–14....172
42:15.........172
42:17.........173

Psalms
1:1............146
3:8............109
6:8............30

6:8–10 33
7:7 109
9:22 109
10:12 109
11:7 110
12:6 109
13 29
13:1–2 28
15:2–4 36
17:15 110
18:4–15 121
18:13–15 129
22 29
22:6–8 21
22:22–27 29
23 94
24:8 .... 123n2
25:4 36
27:4 110
27:12 108
29:2 145
29:3–11 121
32:3–5 17
33:10–11 122
34:21 22
35:10 40
35:11 108
35:19 22
36:9 .... 16n1
37:9 66
38 29
38:3 17
38:5 17
38:21 .... 40n4
40:1–4 28–29
40:5 71
40:9–10 30
44:27 109
51:8 19
55:12–15 28
56:8–11 29
63:3 110
65:8 128

65:9–10 71
68:2 109
71:13 .... 40n4
71:19 40
72:18 166
73 61
74:12–17 121
74:14 151
74:22 109
76:10 109
77:12 166
82:8 109
84:12 158
86:8–9 40
86:10 166
89:9 130
89:9–10 121
89:10 128
89:11 145
89:34 144
90:11 18
92:12–15 131
93:1 145
93:3 130
93:3–4 .... 121, 128
96:6 145
98:1 166
102:10 56
104:1–2 145
104:1–5 126
104:5 126
104:5–9 128
104:10–23 ... 126
104:26 .... 151n7
107:25 121
107:29 121
112 131
119:154 107
128 37
131:1 166
136:4 166
139:21–22 ... 22
148:8 121

Proverbs
3:1–12 .... 37, 131
3:4 158
3:11–12 70
3:33 52
5:19 158
7:13–23 80
15:1 80
23:11 107

Ecclesiastes
2:3 113
2:9 113
8:10 146
10:12 158
12:13 36

Isaiah
6 38
10:1–19 22
13:11 129
13:19 129
14:26 122
17:12–14 121
19:11 122
26:19 .... 109n5
27:1 .... 121, 151
30:10 110
30:30 145
40:26 138
48:9–10 20
51:9–11 ...... 121, 145
51:10 129
51:13 126
63:1 .... 123n2

Jeremiah
5:19 20
5:22 128
6:26 56
10:6–7 40
31:12 30
49:19 .... 123n2
50:34 107
50:44 .... 123n2

Lamentations
3:58–59 107

Ezekiel
16:4 129

Daniel
7:28 67
8:27 67
9 18

Hosea
2:14 27
2:19–20 27
2:20 27

Joel
3:1 67

Micah
7:18 40

Nahum
1:3 121
1:5–6 121

Habakkuk
3:3–15 121
3:14 .... 121, 129

Zechariah
1:7–11 39
3:1–2 44
9:14 121
12:10 158

Matthew
5:44 22
6:22 80

Luke
15:7 19
15:22–24 19
18:13–14 68
19:8 19

John
9:2 19
10:20–22 55
15:20 22

Acts
2:14–41 29
4:24–31 22
12:1–19 21
14:22 11

Romans
5:3 21
5:3–4 19
8:18 22
8:28 .... 11, 157
12:15 91

1 Corinthians
5:4–5 20
5:7 23
8:2–3 102
15:28 45

2 Corinthians
3:17 21
4:16–18 21
4:17 .... 22, 157
11:23–28 21

Galatians
4:9 102
6:7 .... 37, 71

Philippians
3:8 45

Colossians
1:13–14 24
2:15 162

2 Thessalonians
1:4 21
1:6–8 22

2 Timothy
4:17 .... 53n10

Hebrews
10:34 22
11:10 24
11:15–16 24
11:16 26
12:2 159
12:3–11 70
12:4–11 20

James
1:2 21
1:2–4 19
1:22 37
1:26–27 37
1:27 172
5:11 .... 114, 173

1 Peter
1:1 24
1:3–7 22
1:9 46
1:17–18 24
4:12 11
4:12–13 22

2 Peter
1:5 48
1:5–7 21
1:5–8 48
2:11 24

Revelation
2:10 22
4–5 38
12:9 .... 39n4, 154n11
21:1 135
21:1–3 .... 11, 24
21:4 .... 135, 154n11
22:4 110